# Rêvenance

## A Zine of Hauntings from Underground Histories

Issues No. 1 – 5           September 2016 – October 2018

# Omnibus
## Volume I

mOnocle-Lash Anti-Press
2019

**mOnocle-Lash Anti-Press**

**Revenants Series**

monoclelash.wordpress.com
revenant-archive.blogspot.com
monoclelash@gmail.com
bouzingo.blogspot.com

# Contents

# Issue No. 3

# Issue No. 4

## Special Feature: Partymar with the Badouillards!

# Issue No. 5

## Special Feature: Pipelets Under Attack!

# Back (and Forward)

This omnibus contains the first two years of *Rêvenance*: five issues in facsimile, warts and all. While the content is not new (Issue 6 is well underway as I write this!), images are printed here with more clarity than is possible in the zine and the book itself is (relatively) more durable. Furthermore, this volume does contain a few extras likely to be helpful for researchers – and one of the main goals of the journal is for *you*, dear reader, to become or challenge yourself as a researcher, whether on a targeted mission or a delightfully aimless *dérive*. These tools are a complete Table of Contents and index for all five issues.

The latter not only serves navigation but provides full names for people given only surnames in the text, and un-cited authors for books mentioned in the text. It also traces certain themes which have surfaced with some regularity in the journal, often in indirect ways that the index itself even helps bring into relief. I would suggest idly scanning the index as a kind of statistical commentary on the *Rêvenance* project so far, and as a ludic way of reading or re-reading the texts included that is made possible only in their anthologized form. In fact, I found myself inevitably doing so in the laborious process of compiling the index, resulting in some (hopefully) healthy reflection on the journal's first stages, as we move on to new issues.

It has been heartening to see, in re-reading it, not only the large number of contributors and topics, but particularly the many close, real, *personal* relationships that have been revealed among them. Many people and groups turn up repeatedly in un-expected juxtapositions (as the index testifies), revealing a densely-woven social network of counter-cultural activity we have begun to chart. The continuation of this diverse underground realm is shown in the many *kinds* of responses that have appeared: translations, essays, transductions, transcribed facebook exchanges, historiographic poems, anonymous mail art, book reviews, etc.

For all that, the same process of reflection has also turned up areas which have remained unintentionally under-explored or under-developed so far: even granting the demographic realities of 19th Century Europe & America which provide the frame for *Rêvenance's* mandate (the belly of the beast), the roster is still too dominated by straight white men, however radical some of their practices and projects. English and French remain hegemonic here, because I can read them. This is partly a result of a third area for growth: more contributions & collaborations from others! If your language/s, interests, perspectives, or methods diverge from my own, please *give me contributions* to make your voice heard. The Special Features which have developed in Nos. 2 and 3, while not appearing in every issue, will be used to kick-start our incorporation and heightened awareness of some of these issues, including gender fluidity, race, orientalism, etc., among others in keeping with the two so far.

Various practices of experimental *chronicling* – writing the present for future histories – and of what Ed Sanders calls Investigative Poetics – historiography as poetry – have made their appearance in these issues, and I would encourage more vigorous activity in this arena. The same can be said of homophonic transductions and other non-semantic translation and anti-translation methodologies, in dialogue with the more traditional translations.

The zine's founding manifesto can be read on page 3 of the first issue. I launched *Rêvenance* with the assumption that it would somehow manage to be even *more* esoteric than mOnocle-Lash's already notoriously "unpublishable" output – crazy cultural radicals are rare enough, but crazy cultural radicals anxious to recognise and learn from what was radical two centuries ago...? Much to my surprise and gratification, it turns out there are more of us than I had thought: the journal has become the press's biggest seller. (Many dozens of copies!!!) I have been encouraged and entered into stimulating dialogues with independent researchers, writers, teachers, activists, publishers, and translators across a broad spectrum of subcultures and perspectives: avant-gardists and mail-art networkers; punk, noise, and free improv scenes; fandom and bibiliophilic communities; zine fests; and many more.

Proof, one hopes, that even as we behold the impending tipping-points of the political and socio-economic (not to mention ecological) horrors that so many of us in these nether-regions of capitalist civilisation have been warning against *for generations* (as these pages show), the heterogeneous community of ontological revolt is still alive and capable of struggle and adaptation. Let it proceed armed with the knowledge of *what we have been* – an inimitable tradition in which continuity and memory takes the very form of fluidity and novelty – so that we may face the harsh future with the joyful cunning to forge *what we shall be.*


Olchar E. Lindsann
Editor, *Rêvenance.*

# Rêvenance

## A Zine of Hauntings from Underground Histories

Issue No. 1                                September 2016 (A.Da. 100, A.H. 186)

### Featuring

**The Dead**: Alphonse Allais / Georges d'Heylli / Alphonse Karr / Gérard de Nerval / Charles Nodier / Maurice Rollinat / Michel Roly / Francis Vielé-Griffin

**The Living**: Raymond E. Andé III / John M. Bennett / Peter Ciccariello / Michael Helsem / Gleb Kolomiets / Edward Kulemin / Jim Leftwich / Olchar E. Lindsann

Writer, performer and organiser **Edward Kulemin**, co-founder of KEPNOS, the Group of Unknown Artists, the Smolensk School of Apologists, and other collectives, has exerted an important influence on his own and subsequent generations of the Russian avant-garde. His visual responses to cultural history, placed throughout the issue, are part of the same vibrant tradition of Russian visual writing and transrational language that was pioneered by the Russian Futurists and the Zoum collectve, and is also represented by Rea Nikonova, discussed in pp. 19–24. Early experiments in this direction include those by Charles Nodier in 1830 (see p. 30)

~^~^~^~^~^~^~^~^~

**Edited by Olchar E. Lindsann**

Sept., A.Da. 100
A.H. 176
2016 A.D.

**mOnocle-Lash Anti-Press**
monoclelash.wordpress.com
monoclelash@gmail.com

**Revenants Series**
revenant-archive.blogspot.com
bouzingo.blogspot.com

**Apollo Concept**
*by Edward Kulemin*

# Forward (and Back)

*Rêvenance* promotes history practiced as game, as social necromancy, as activism, as dream (fr., *rêve)*, as trans-generational collaboration, as communal memory: a historiography that runs athwart the academic, refuses to describe history as dead, as finished, which does not stand apart to observe its object from a distance, in the posture of false 'objectivity' which Power always assumes. Instead: a *committed* historiography, which does not claim to stand outside the stream of time or apart from its object, intellectual and precise, yet ludic and multi-form, one moment manifest as an essay, the next as a poem; a historiography researched and written *from within* the utopian fringe, and *for* the same community, responsive to our changing conditions, needs, and desires; history as a communal dream of something intimately *other* within itself. A historiography that *we take personally*, which merges imperceptibly into daily life, thought, embodied dissent, and continued experimental practice and life.

Like the Revenant imprint and archive, this journal will focus on forgotten and newly-discovered histories of avant-garde, radical activist, utopian, and other underground countercultures. While the primary focus will be on the 19th Century, earlier and later material is also welcome, and contributions that directly connect counter-cultural movements and strategies across time are particularly encouraged. The primary goal is to explore histories, communities, and themes that are not consistently represented elsewhere. *Rêvenance* seeks to develop a community of independent DIY researchers who see historical work as part of a communal praxis directed toward contemporary and future change; it is a laboratory in which countercultural history is transmuted, reflected and disseminated in the current lifestyle, writing, music, art, and thought of present-day communities of dissent or otherness.

There is a small but ardent sprinkling of us across the world whose varied interests have led us to converge, via different paths, upon an overlapping cluster of historical subjects, and who are activating that history within an array of subcultures from the Avant-Garde to Fanfic to Punk to Decadence to Weird Fiction; a lot of knowledge and reflection, which has scarcely been shared or made visible. Ideally, the journal's readers will also be its contributors; with time, we will find our separate areas of research connecting and reinforcing each other.

We welcome all forms of historical engagement: essays, translations, sample passages of books and images in the public domain, transductions & re-workings of old work, poems (think Ed Sanders' Investigative Poetics, Banville's poems on Romanticism), book reviews, stories (romans à clefs? speculative fanfic?), bibliographies and reading-lists, historiographic theory, and more. Much of this material may be drawn upon for later re-publication in anthologies by Revenant Editions, or expanded to full chapbooks. It will consistently feature passages and translations taken from the Revenant Archive, and research relating to it and the *Resurrecting the Bouzingo* project.

This first issue indicates the potential range of our collective enquiry and approach: an essay on subversive historiography by Russian avant-gardist Gleb Kolomiets, translations of Decadent poetry by contemporary dark dandy Raymond E. Andre III, an experimental transduction by avant-poet & publisher John M. Bennett of a frenetic poet and a working-class socialist activist from the 19th Century, pictographic meditations by the experimental poet Edward Kulemin, straightforward translations of Romanticist verse, avant-garde Volapük texts from 1890 (Vielé-Griffin) and today (Michael Helsem), and a facebook discussion thread linking the late 20th Century Russian visual poet Rea Nikonova with the early 20th Century painter Malevich and the late 19th Century *Incoherents* group. I have also included the Forwards from the inaugural issues of two small 19th Century journals that have served as partial models and inspirations for *Rêvenance*. Future issues will expand on radical politics, occultism, utopian experimentation, gender-play, racial equity, and other dimensions.

*Rêvenance* is a conversation, a scrapbook, a walking corpse, an arsenal, a reliquary, a warning, a game, a weapon, a rotting box unearthed in a deserted garret, a dream or nightmare, a return of the repressed. It is the dead returned to earth to play; and also to set things aflame.

**Olchar E. Lindsann**

*The word 'zine' in the subtitle is a reminder that we desire participation above all, and encourage contributions that are humble in size, but striking in their interest or intriguing in their implications. I particularly encourage short essays , micro-essays, and translations—we'd rather have a couple paragraphs on a fascinating subject than nothing at all because you haven't the time to write something longer.*

*The journal will be published on an irregular basis, whenever enough contributions accumulate and I have time to print. Submissions will be rolling: send me what you have when it's ready, and it will go into the next issue. Email contributions or questions to monoclelash@gmail.com or olindsann@gmail.com.*

# CONTENTS

*Many of the source texts are available online at gallica.bnf.fr and/or at archive.org. Supplements with source texts will accompany future issues.*

**Cover image by Olchar E. Lindsann**, collaged from: Célestin Nanteuil, *Portrait of Alphonse Karr* (1838), Grandville, Cover to Karr's *Les Guêpes* (1839), Tony Johannot, illustrations from Nodier's *Sept Chateaux du Roi de Bohême* (1830/52), Cham, cartoon of an anarchist bookshop from *Études sociales* (1848) & Colophon from the *Gazette Anecdotique* (1876). All constituent images are photocopied from original editions held in the Revenant Archive.

*Gleb Kolomiets is extremely active in the contemporary Russian avant-garde, as writer, theorist, publisher, translator, organiser, curator, and historian. He is the editor of the journal **Slova**, an important point of international exchange among radical, anti-commercial creative workers; founder of the decentralized underground press **Mycelium**; and has organised many cultural events in Smolensk and elsewhere, including the **First Russian Asemic Exhibit**.*

# What Governs the History of Art? (2016)

*Gleb Kolomiets*

In our daily experience we often observe how history becomes an instrument of power - the works of historians end up as transmitters of the state and religious propaganda, tools of the market or the media for the public opinion. It seems that history easily submits to the outside influences; its structure in some way facilitates implantation of external elements not related to cognition.

Indeed, the history, if we understand it as a narration on events, evidence and material objects in accordance with a certain time interval, is inevitably subordinated not only to the linear structure of speech or writing, but also the linear structure of time. Even at this level of the organization, we find the power relations - the objects of historical narrative are in a subordinate position to the general rules of the organization of narrative and time. And this power can be considered a political, as time management and control of the narrative are also the ways of managing people (working hours, personal history as a social role).

Is it possible to make the history of art immune to the incoming impulses of the political influence? I do not think so, because it would require establishing of the history which has no relation to time or description of events. However, since history is so easy to manage, may it be possible to reclaim the historical narrative for personal needs or for needs of a community? If it is impossible to emancipate history of art, maybe we can make sure that it does not serve politics, market, or society in general?

To answer these questions, we need to consider the exact power relations established within the historical narrative. By taking control of the points where subjection of the history takes place, we *probably* may be able to protect the entire structure from control by the forces we oppose.[1]

---

[1] I have written "probably" because our unconscious is constantly influenced by the major political and social structures, thus while reclaiming history for ourselves, we can unwittingly become the agents of power. However, this should not stop us, since any experiment, even carried out under the strictest control, can bring unexpected and beneficial results.

Describing these "points of subjection" I will deliberately avoid their classification, as classification itself is a way to establish power relations. From a tactical point of view, it would be more effective to describe them in arbitrary order, as if I am watching the behavior of an animal or human and describing his behavior as it appeared in a natural way.

1. *Temporal organization.* The concept of historical period determined the structure of the modern history of art (Wolfflin) and opened numerous opportunities to for the political influences. It is easy to build a hierarchy of the events arranged in certain order and generalized under the basic concept of period. And it is easy to give the hierarchy ideological content. Therefore, while reclaiming the history for personal purposes, it is important to pay attention to the concept of time we use. The linear time is not the only possibility. One can use a circular scheme or describe the events while taking in account their substantial incompleteness (when we do not separate the events from what is called their consequences and describe the past like what is occurs now), or to try to find our own concepts of time.

2. *Composition of narrative.* It is impossible to coin a narrative without an organization. Every story has a beginning, middle and end. The academic history is subject to criteria of the scientific narrative, to the requirements of the so-called objectivity. When we reclaim the history for ourselves, we must keep distance from the ideological forms of narrative. For example, Vasari showed that the history of art can be made up of subjective stories about individuals, about life of the artists. Since then, biography has become a tool of subjection of the history by market (non-fiction biographies of the artists and writers as a commercial product), however, this does not prevent us from the search of hidden emancipative potentials of biography. In addition, we can adopt the narrative practices which were used by the avant-garde literature and visual art (The Nouveau Roman, cut-up, asemic writing etc.). The inclusion of the author into the narrative can be an effective way of resistance to the "spirit of objectivity" of the academic history.

3. *Totalization.* General concepts such as style, movement, form, iconography and other define the modern art history. The generalization of historical figures,

events and movements under control of the general notion automatically arranges their hierarchy, and that allows dividing primary from secondary, significant from insignificant, mainstreaming from marginal, and thus controlling a reader's attention. It is a way of elimination or marginalization of the "inconvenient" aspects of the history in order to transform its overall picture into something consistent with the interests of the authorities. Therefore, while reclaiming the history, in my opinion, one should avoid these generalizations. There are a lot of alternative concepts ready for use: community or network; rhizome, plateau, plane or chaosmos (Deleuze and Guattari); multitude (Hardt and Negri). And there is a good tactical opportunity here for the invention of the concepts of our own. The main point is to use concepts that resist hierarchy and refer to the decentralized structures.

4. *Causal relationships.* Back in the 18th century David Hume dealt a crushing blow to the concept of causality by showing that its explanatory power is much overrated. However, scientists and philosophers still continue to fight actively for the restoration of the power of causality. Indeed, the binary division of events and the idea that one of them is derived from the other allows you to create rigid conceptual structure with the powerful relationships of subordination. And this technique was adopted by art history. As a consequence of the establishment of causality we can unfold a genealogy of styles, state the impact of context on art and vice versa or isolate the determining factors of the historical process in art. It is better to avoid the establishment of causal relationships while reclaiming the history for yourself, or at least assert their probabilistic nature.

5. *Context.* Judging from my experience, description of the context is mainly used for finding the cause-and-effect relationships. Impact of the situation, the impact of the zeitgeist, the influence of circumstances - everything is at the service of casual hierarchies. However, the context has value in itself, because it allows the control of the range of interpretations of artworks and management of the search for overt and covert allusions. In this case, the context becomes an attention management tool. In terms of resistance to power, there are two possible tactics: either achievement of maximum completeness of the disclosure of the context, so that the reader's attention covers the entire range

of possible interpretations, or, conversely, the complete elimination of the context from the historical narrative and description of the history of art as an isolated and autonomous sphere of reality.

So these are the points of subjection of the art history. They can be perceived as a kind of strategic resource of a revolutionary. As in 1917 Bolsheviks began the destruction of the tsarist regime with the capture of post and telegraph, so now non-academic historians can start fighting with pro-government history with takeover of these strategic positions. The point is to learn the "lessons of history" and recall the results of the Bolshevik Revolution, to make sure that the seizure of power does not give birth to a totalitarian regime.

*The **Gazette anecdotique, littéraire, artistique et bibliographique (Anecdotal, Litterary, Artistic and Bibliographic Gazette)** was published from the 1870s into the first years of the 20th Century, and was aimed at cultural historians, archivists, and others involved in Romanticist and post-Romanticist history. It was edited and mostly written by Georges d'Heylli, chief archivist of the Comédie française, who also published a dictionary of literary pseudonyms and a collection of documents related to the Paris Commune. The **Gazette Anecdotique** has served as one of the principal inspirations for **Revenance**, not least due to Heylli's hope that his readers would be his principle contributors.*

# Forward
## to the Anecdotal, Literary, Artistic, and Bibliographic Gazette (1876)
### *by Georges d'Heylli*

The very title of our new publication sufficiently indicates its aim and spirit. We wish to give, two times a month, a quick story of the fortnight as recounted by curious events, new or forgotten, anecdotes, biographical details, documents, in a word, all the particularities that can extend interest. We also want to collect or point out, in choosing them from amongst the best, the thousand daily stories, the relevant letters, the articles or fragments of articles most marked by various points of view—politics excepted—sowed from day to day, and as quickly vanished, in the journals of Paris or province. One can not imagine, in fact, the amount of vigor and spirit which is expended, at the same time as the number of curiosities of all kinds which are thus lost.

We will make an equal place for bibliography, as much to point out new books as to provide literary and biographical notes concerning them. The theatre, finally, shall not pass forgotten either in our publication, and the performance of new pieces will furnish us both with the occasion for information on their authors and on their interpreters.

This statement constitutes the programme of that which we shall call the "contemporary" part of the *Anecdotal Gazette*; but our intention is then to complete each issue with a series of retrospective, unpublished, or forgotten documents.

Our readers can, moreover, themselves help us greatly with this last aspect of our little journal, and pass along to us — in original or in copy — the interesting pieces that they consider appropriate to offer publicity. Our collection would not know how, in fact, to find better collaborators than our readers and subscribers themselves.

Similar publications to our own have already been made in recent years. We refer especially to the *Anecdotal Review* of Lorédan Larchey, the *Little Review* published by Pincebourde, the *Pocket Review* of Albert Millaud, the *Retrospective Revue* of d'Avrecourt, etc... We were certainly inspired by the spirit and example of these inventive publications, vanished today, bringing nonetheless all possible improvements, as much in content as in form, in this new collection that we embark upon.

January 15, 1876

*Translated by Olchar E. Lindsann*

from *Gazette anecdotique, littéraire, artistique et bibliographique*. Year 1, No. 1: Jan. 15, 1876. ed. Georges d'Heylli. Librairie des Bibliophiles, Paris.

*Gustave Karr's self-published satirical magazine* **Les Guêpes** *(The Wasps) was a milestone in the history of avant-garde and DIY publishing. After the Revolution of 1830, the new moderate-liberal Monarchy exercised effective censorship through economic rather than political means, destroying the artist- and activist-run Small Press community in favour of a few huge corporate press conglomerates, as Karr describes here. In response he started this self-published venture (which lasted ten years) with an intentionally tiny audience. This move was*

*extremely rare at the time, when printing technology was expensive and inaccessible, over a century before the 'Mimeograph Revolution', and Karr's rationale in this essay for self-publishing as political and literary dissent, shows him laying the very early groundwork upon which 'zine and micropress publishing would eventually emerge. Karr's discourse in each issue swerves and merges unpredictably, almost as if by stream of consciousness, between political tirades, comedy sketches, gossip and in-jokes about the avant-garde community, literary and social criticism, and sarcastic observations about daily life. The series was re-issued in 1853 under the newly-installed dictator Napoleon III, but redacted for its political outspokenness. After an abortive attempt to re-start the journal, Karr ceased writing, refusing to do so under a totalitarian regime, and devoted the rest of his life to botany.*

## The Wasps (1839 & 1853)

### I. Introduction to Redacted 1853 edition:

The history recounted by the *Wasps* encases a period of ten years.

Of this collection, completely unavailable in bookstores, they asked me for a new edition.

I would consider my integrity concerned not to make any changes, either in the ideas, nor in the judgements, —even had my ideas and my judgements changed, —which they have not.

Only a few pages have been suppressed, at the demand of the editors, —we could not have printed today that which we spoke at the time, —and I do not wish to speak otherwise.

I shall reread the hundred volumes of *Wasps*, and, in my conscience, I can repeat today that which I stated at the top of the first volume, published in November 1839.

*A.K.*
*April 1853*

~~~~~~~~~~~~~~~~~~~~~

### Preface, Warning, Forward;
### All of It in Twenty Lines (1839 Forward)

This little book is the first of twelve such volumes which shall appear successively each month, between now and a year hence.

They shall contain frank and inexorable expression of my thought on men and on things exclusive of any idea of ambition, of any party influence.

I would speak without rage, because in my eyes the most spiteful men are even more ridiculous than spiteful, and incidentally I am certain that they also make at the same time more harm and more regret.

I do not belong to any party: I judge things as they occur, men as they appear; I take few things seriously, because, having no need of anyone but my friends, and not demanding their friendship from them, I feel, I see and I judge with the detachment and tranquil cheerfulness of a reasonably well-seated spectator.

I address my little books *to the unknown friends* whom I can have in the world, to the gentlemen of good sense and of spirit: that is to say that I took measures in order not to require but a small number of subscribers.

We laugh well together at gentlemen who would wish to pass as serious, and we amuse ourselves by measuring the pettiness of *great* men and of *great* things.

---

*November 1839*

Certainly, to people who know me as a man of leisure and fantasy, it must seem extraordinary that I should go thus, with lightness of heart, to give myself the bother and ennui to create a publication, when there appear every morning under the ambitious heading of *organs* of *public opinion*, such a great quantity of squares of paper, wherein it would be permissible for me to slide whatever I might have to say to my contemporaries.

It must therefore be that I had a strong and invincible reason, and that reason is here:

It is that *there is not* ONE *journal in which one could put twenty lines where it would be neither foolish, nor in bad faith.* I take it to a number of witnesses, men of spirit and of talent, who write there or rather who struggle there against such ennui and bad taste. I do better, I prove.

As least as I recall it, in the month of July of the year 1830, a revolution was made *for freedom of the press* by that interesting part of the population which does not know how to read: the press is thus free.

If despotism has its inconveniences, liberty has its own too; despotism is regarded by those who exercise it, either as a law, or as a power acquired by force, and consequently odious[2]: like law, it has limits, like all law, outside of which it would cease to exist; like usurpation, there is a drop that one dares not put into the cup at the risk of making it overflow.

But liberty having one virtue, it takes its most gruesome or its most grotesque excesses for progress, and it does not recognise limits.

The government thought to act wisely, in putting *some* restrictions on liberty of the press.

These few restrictions fill in the Code eleven pages, each and every one containing fifty lines of sixty letters, that is to say around seventy pages of an ordinary volume.

The government thought to act wisely, in which it is perfectly misguided.

The press without shackles served as counter-weight to itself; every nuance had its journal, and each journal had but a small number of readers.

The caution-money[3] was the greatest shackle, but at the same time it created privileges; that is to say that, if it made many journals impossible, it gave immense power to those which could fulfill its conditions, in that the diverse nuances of readers were absorbed into one colour and made for each of the existing journals a too-numerous readership.

The fiscal conditions imposed upon the press removed them from the hands of writers in order to put them into those of speculators and entrepreneurs.

Thus, today, on cannot cite a single writer-owner of a journal; but, in revenge, the press is governed, directed by old hatmakers, old pharmacists, old lawyers, etc.; by a few,—the journals by stock-shares,—belong at the same time to two thousand grocers, bootmakers, pastry-chefs, haberdashers, meat-roasters, porters, wigmakers, butchers, barristers—and other citizens of a dubious literature.

Here are the results of this order of things for the government and for the writers.

The government, by one of those blunders which none but governments would

---

2  "le despotisme est considéré par celui qui l'exerce, ou comme un droit, ou comme une puissance acquise par la force, et conséquemment odieuse;"

3  After the Restoration Monarchy was overthrown in 1830 in the name of a Free Press and other (largely unfulfilled) grievances, the Cautionnement, or Caution-Money, was instituted by the Liberal monarchy that took control, in order to control the political opposition on both left and right without direct censorship. This was a large monetary deposit paid in advance by the publisher, to act as 'security' against any future charges of sedition or political agitation that might later be filed against the journal. For a detailed analysis, see Jeremy D. Popkin, Press, Revolution, and Social Identities in France, 1830-1835, passim.

know how to commit, made to pass the weapon which it feared in the hands of poets into the hands of businessmen and merchants. The merchants know what they put into and what they risk in an enterprise, and multiply the earnings by the risks that should return this money to them. They have a stability, a pertinacity, that the writers have never had, these who have never had in view ideas, paradoxes[4] or systems. The merchants go straight to their goal, which is to bleed the government dry as friend or as foe, or to topple it in order to take or sell its place. You wanted to have business with the merchants; well then! settle yourself with them; they buy the press from you in bulk, they sell it back to you in retail, and shall make a profit on it, and they shall sell it to you expensively, and they shall pay you entirely with that which is yours, and of a good many things which are not yours.

For the gentlemen of letters, who speak so highly and so often of their independence, here is what they gained from *progress*. They are no more, it is true, paid wages by Louis XIV; they lift the head proudly and sympathise with or misunderstand Corneille, who suffered this shameful yoke; but they are paid wages by Mr. Third-Etate, bargaining in wine, or making smokestacks, or two thousand bootmakers, meat-roasters, porters, barristers, etc., of whom I was speaking to you just now, who deposited the caution-money of a one-hundred-thousand francs required by law.

<@> There are but two kinds of journals: those which approve and prop up the government, whatever it should do, and those which blame and attack it, whatever it should do. That the government should take two *contradictory* measures, something neither impossible nor rare: it is clear that if the one is bad, the second is good. Oh well! *There is not a single journal* where on can say this.

<@> The journals of the opposition are just as servile in their criticism as the ministerial journals in their enthusiasm.

<@> Aside from these obvious drawbacks, there are other more hidden ones.

One such independent journal, usually hostile to power, soften their colours each time that a royal theatre fails to renew the contract of a certain skinny dancer.

<@> Another such, always candid with admiration in front of the youngest sons of the Bureau of Ministers, mix a little absinthe in their honey, a certain times when it is the custom to discuss the subsidies given to the journals.

Just as in no journal can one express one's whole thought, there is for the gentle-

---

4   "Paradox" in underground Romanticist slang signified a conceptual formulation in which logic was used to create or support an impossible or self-contradictory proposition — a forerunner of pata-physical reasoning.

men who have no ambition, and therefore retain good sense and good faith, there is[5] one drawback which prevents from uniting with any of the parties in possession of the press.

The governmental party, to judge by its bosses[6], has the advantage over the opposition party. It possesses men of real science, experience, true spirit and good company; but it drags behind it every one of the beggars, valets and bigots.

The opposition party presents with a just pride gentlemen of resolution and even devotion, gentlemen of severe and tested integrity; but its tail is formed of all of the slacking womanizers of the cafés, the rowdy, the bums, the spineless,[7] armchair terrorists.

And the commendable men of the two parties know how cumbersome and difficult these tails are to drag around.

< @ > There does not exist in France a single journal which would dare to print complete in their columns the present little book. It is not however because it holds anything which should be contrary to the law, to public morality, and good sense — praise God, they do not watch so closely here.

*Translated by Olchar E. Lindsann*

***from:***
*Les Guêpes*, Nov., 1839. Ed. & Written by Alphonse Karr. Self-Published, Paris.
&
Alphonse Karr, *Les Guêpes: Première Série. Nouvelle édition.* 1887. 2nd Ed. Calmann Lévy, Paris. Three Volumes.

~^~^~^~^~^~^~^~^~^~^~^~^~^~^~^~^~^~^~^~^~^~^~^~^~^~^~^~^~^~^~^~

---

5   sic.
6   "sommités"
7   "fainéants coureurs d'estaminets, de tapageurs, de braillards, de vauriens, de *colotteurs de pipes.*" Karr is indulging in a number of neologisms and apparently unconventional usages here; my current translation of "colutteurs de pipe"—technically "those who wear pants signifying support of the Reign of Terror who sit around smoking pipes"—as "armchair terorists" is pretty loose and I welcome suggested improvements.

*Michel Roly was a carpenter active in the French Socialist network around 1840. Little is known of him; he was probably self-taught, and printed his poetry in radical workers' journals such as* **La Ruche populaire**. *His poem "The Bee" was published in an anthology of Socialist workers' poetry edited by Olinde Rodrigues, a key organiser and theorist of Saint-Simonist socialism and the coiner of the term 'Avant-Garde' as taken up (probably with his encouragement) by radicalised elements within Romanticist subculture. John M. Bennett has produced a homophonic transduction of the poem, favouring the transmission of sound over semantics.*

## Obey

*Transduction by John M. Bennett*

A pair of furious vents' dull hoard,
Surprise a loin's jar of republic sot,
One obeys joy's dull sort,
Isolated melancholic eats,
Sued the mortared cum unbent:
The car's iced bad, sandy ether's futile,
The vile east, dizzy hell, a foot's bent present;
What sorts my low desire: my jerky piss careened in vain?
Oh meal distiller, what sordid cake abstains my junk?
Junk nor reconnoitered piss danced trussed's cess climactic,
Mooned the humble packrat, such simple eglantine;
Jesus' vain church the pus ledger rapes.
Awesome Freud abstinence ate,
Bent the vent, and the hatted moon triped;
Oh grey day mist desires, terminal maw of sufferance!
Hell dips: quandered Phoebus, dumb bean-flavored rayon,
The rechuffed Satan, renacred fits in sounded choir
The tent's duped appearance,
Its courage ardor ate.
Lore's changing language day,
Notorious obeyed, in ceaseless moths, addressed the Toot-Pissed
(or Pluto or Sol, said senseless pus image):
"Lass! What recoinage pours the coughing moon's chorus?
See scenic promise assured, eat a sincere
Days' chanchre makes the vile empire
A horror that ate the less human servants."

Fiddled piss is the ceaseless voice, the feeble creature
Descried danced the airs, saw fried chimney sense:
"A mind touted the flowers nature produced,
Oily roses, but ate the jasmin;
Ate voiced, sure teeth, whose nasal sand cultured
Day's mist larceny, loin of chagrined voices,
Vexed and delicious joy's
Oval mind a chalice evokes!
Ceaseless poured OM and Dew poured butter jerk in veins!
Apprentice car, belled mist tooth,
Clay pursed hour of day's novels;
Voice received a suck whose day's pawed mortals
Put on calm less dollars, appraised the suffering;
Ate the sheer clumped jaw, lurid dance recoined,
An ill broiled sore's the author's
Dull creator of the celestial throat."
Or, is't a pendulant sea discourse all borders quells,
A stacked floor offers sordid route
To Hell's tall buttered ossuary;
Sea which fits a bent labor neutered
Suspended in sun's pissoir,
Divined pensive and saucy...
Or disposed to precocious treasure sounds?
Maze of sound's doom clock's a vapid scene o'erlaid:
What face sees brute?  Sees a bombed village,
Envious asshole obeyed
A venous table sees trouble eat, sees laws
Suck off a brief illness veined with deconstructed lore.
A notorious heroine defines the respite,
Which, the treatment sore, recuts its danced sound said,
Jerked to finish the sand's dazed commentary.
Blinking, expect to obey said mind,
The village says toil;
Toil for veins' elevation, to choke on *Popular Rust;*
*Is this my offered sound's turbulence abraded?*

*A Transduction of "L'Abeille" by Michel Roly, in*
*Poésies Sociales des Ouvriers, Réunies et Publiées par*
*Olinde Rodrigues, Paris: Paulin, Libraire, 1841.*

~^~^~^~^~^~^~^~^~^~^~^~^~^~^~^~^~^~^~^~^~^~^~^~^~^~^~^~^~^~^~^~

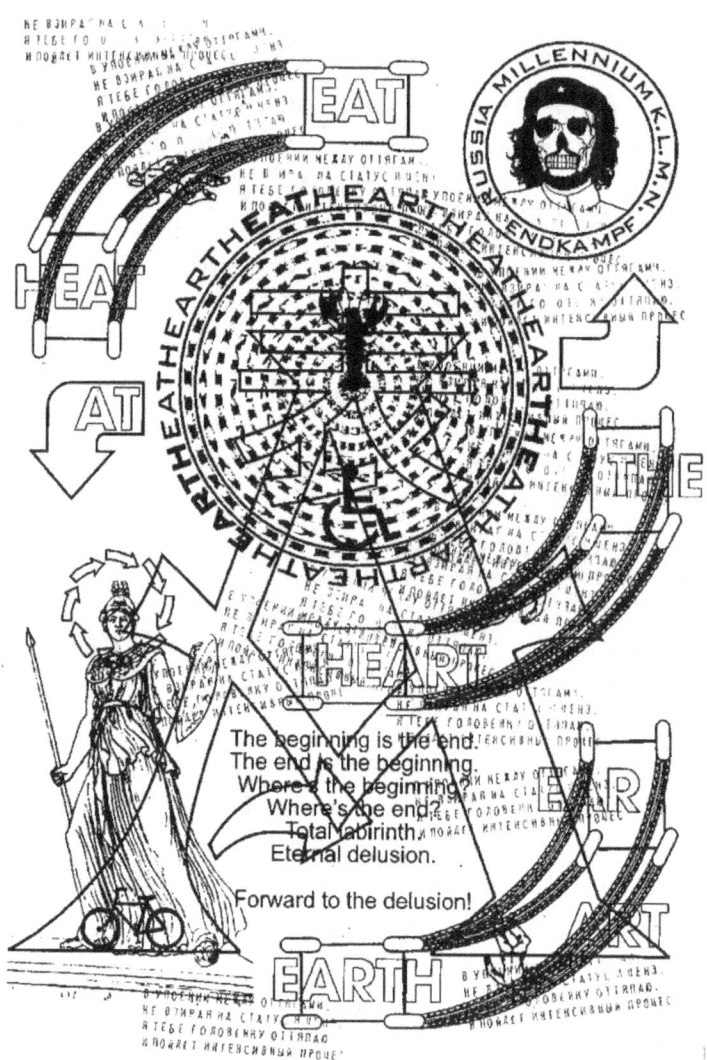

by Edward
Kulemin

*This conversation is snared from a facebook post and comment-thread by the American avant-gardists Leftwich, Ciccariello, and Bennett (see Bennett's transductions elsewhere in this issue) on June 9, 2016. In it, a discussion about the Russian visual poet Rea/Ry Nikonova leads inexorably back to the late 19th Century, via some interesting routes.*

## A Thread: From Nikonova to the Incoherents (2016)
*by Jim Leftwich, Peter Ciccariello, & John M.* Bennett

Linda Nochlin, from "The Invention of the Avant-Garde: France, 1830-1880"
in *The Avant-Garde*, edited by Thomas B. Hess & John Ashbery; published in 1968
https://msu.edu/course/ha/446/nochlinavant-garde.pdf

> "The very term "avant-garde" was first used figuratively to designate radical or advanced activity in both the artistic and social realms. It was in this sense that it was first employed by the French Utopian socialist Henri de Saint-Simon, in the third decade of the nineteenth century, when he designated artists, scientists, and industrialists as the elite leadership of the new social order:
>
> It is we artists who will serve you as avant-garde [Saint-Simon has his artist proclaim, in an imaginary dialogue between the latter and a scientist] ... the power of the arts is in fact most immediate and most rapid: when we wish to spread new ideas among men, we inscribe them on marble or on canvas."

Nochlin found the Saint-Simon quote in an essay by Donald D. Egbert, published in 1967 in The American Historical Review. He says he's the first to point out that this particular usage of the term "avant-garde" can be traced back to Saint-Simon.

from The Idea of "Avant-Garde" in Art and Politics:
> "It has never previously been pointed out, I believe, that the figurative use of the word avant-garde to denote radically progressive leaders of both art and society [...] can be traced to Henri de Saint-Simon (1760 - 1825)."

http://web.stanford.edu/group/orbisafrica/Latinamerican/PDF-ARCHIVE_files/0-150%202.pdf

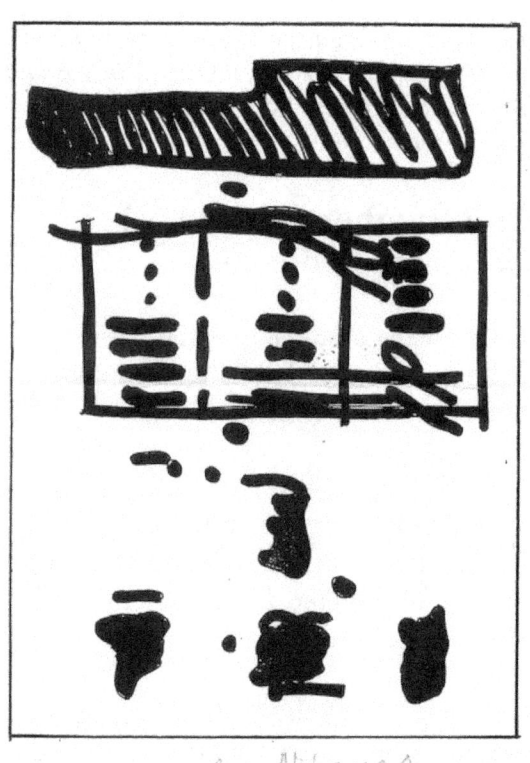

Rea Nikonova: *page 19 & 20: http://dare.uva.nl/document/2/30565*

[PALIMPSESTS. VISUAL POETRY BY RY NIKONOVA AND SERGEJ SIGEJ, vy C. Greve (2004)

*Thee Black Square Inn the visual poetry of Ry Nikonova*, Kazimir Malevichs Black Square plays an important role as an icon of the ideal synthesis of literature and painting. The Black Square is seen as the ultimate palimpsest, as the supreme finality of all literature: :

(If one regards the masterpiece of the Black Square as a literary collapse which contains all words of all times and peoples, then turning again to a verbal sphere becomes superfluous.) (Nikonova 1998:82)

This is most plainly visualized in her poem 'Transponirovanie kartiny K. Malevichaa v cernyj bespauznyj stich' (Transposition of K. Malevich' Picture to a Black Poem without Spaces'). However, a potential transgression of thee Black Square emerges in the thinning of the edges of this visual poem resulting from an apparently arbitrary transgression of the geometrical lines of the square by blurry unstructured letters. Thus, it can also be seen as a reservoir of potential:

[The colossal potential accumulated by this "black gap" of art can collapse into a dot, evaporate to a white square, to the vacuum art of a platform [...] or it can simply grow vectors of energy.) One possibility, therefore, is to reveal the so-called energies hidden in the black geometrical form. These are realized as vectors springing out from the geometrical form, leading apparently no-where at times.]

(Nikonova and Sigej 1990)

*Jim Leftwich*: "If one regards the masterpiece of the Black Square as a literary collapse which contains all words of all times and peoples, then turning again to a verbal sphere becomes superfluous." -Nikonova

*Peter Ciccariello*: And if not?

*Jim Leftwich*: If one does not regard the masterpiece of the Black Square as a literary collapse which contains all words of all times and peoples, then turning again to a verbal sphere does not become superfluous.

*Peter Ciccariello*: Interesting link, in the sense that the square would be the logical extension of abstract at the time. https://news.artnet.com/.../kizimir-male-vich-black-square...

Shocking Insights into Malevich's 'Black Square' - artnet News, NEWS.ARTNET.COM

["It was known that under the Black Square, there was some underlying image," Ekaterina Voronina, an art researcher at the Tretyakov told *Kultura TV*. "We found out that there is not one image, but two."

She continued, "We proved that the initial image is a Cubo-Futurist composition, while the painting lying directly under the Black Square—the colors of which you can see in the cracks—is a proto-Suprematist composition."

The x-ray analysis also uncovered a handwritten note by the artist on the painting's white border which is still being deciphered. However, according to AFP, preliminary investigations have revealed that the text says "Negroes battling in a cave."

The note may be a reference to an 1897 black square painting by the French writer Alphonse Allais titled Combat des Negres dans une cave, pendant la nuit ("Negroes Fighting in a Cellar at Night.")

If the preliminary interpretation holds up, it could support a connection to the earlier French painting, demonstrating that one of Malevich's most famous works was in fact an art historical response or an interpretation of Allais's piece, showing that the Russian artist's pool of influences had been much broader than previously thought.]

*Malevich, Black Square*

*John M. Bennett*: The actual painting is full of brush strokes and subtle variations

*Peter Ciccariello*: A black square is not a black square. I remember standing in front of it for an inordinate amount of time aware of tiny explosions of color from the black field to the margin.

*John M. Bennett*: yes indeed

*Jim Leftwich*: I love the connection to the Incoherents group

   The Incoherents:

1882, the poet Paul Bilhaud exhibited Combat de négres dans une cave, pendant la nuit (Negroes fighting in a cellar at night)

1883, Alphonse Allais exhibited Première communion de jeunes filles chlorotiques par un temps de neige (First Communion of Anaemic Girls in the Snow)

1884, Alphonse Allais exhibited Récolte de la tomate par des cardinaux apoplectiques au bord de la mer Rouge (Apoplectic Cardinals Harvesting Tomatoes by the Shores of the Red Sea)

Later Allais published a book of these and other similar works, which also included Marche funèbre composée pour les funérailles d'un grand homme sourd (Funeral March for the Obsequies of a Deaf Man)

*John M. Bennett*: formidable!

*Peter Ciccariello*: fabulous!
   I think I need to be an incoherent from now on.

*Incoherent works by Alphonse Allais*

~^~^~^~^~^~^~^~^~^~^~^~^~^~^~^~^~^~^~^~^~^~^~^~^~^~^~^~^~^~

*The avant-comedian Alphonse Allais, discussed above, was one of the most active writers and organisers of the Incoherents group, and later of the* **Chat Noir,** *with many of the same collaborators. He performed at the famous cabaret and co-edited its journal. The* **Chat Noir** *was one of the few places where avant-garde subculture genuinely merged with popular culture, and Allais is still highly regarded in France, though obscure in the anglophone world. Revenant Editions is currently preparing a chapbook of his work.*

## Some Figures (1893)
### *by Alphonse Allais*

Terront emerged as victor of the match known by the name of the *Terront-Corre Match*, after having *covered* a thousand kilometers in 41 hours 58 minutes 52 4/5 seconds.

A parenthesis, i.y.p.[8]

(Some uninitiated readers have written to me from the provinces to request a hint on this expression *covered*. Why do we say *he has covered* instead of *he has travelled?*

The explanation is spicy enough.

It is Mr. Porel, the clever ex-director of Eden, with the real name of Parfourou, who prevailed upon the cycling authorities to replace the word *travelled* with the word *covered*, in order to avoid the inevitably regrettable confusions.

Close the parenthesis, i.y.p. )

Since I had nothing to do this morning, I busied myself with some calculations.

1,000 kilometers in 41 hours 58 minutes 52 4/5 seconds, that puts the kilometer at 19 seconds and 12 tierces (the tierce is quite a small measurement rarely used in everyday life, which corresponds to one sixtieth of a second), and the meter to 1 tierce and some change.

I have not pursued it right up to the millimeter, such calculation seeming pointless to me. It would, indeed, be quite strange never to attempt to record the millimeter.

This pleasant speed, quite respectable for a cyclist, becomes almost ridiculous if we compare it to the speed of light (77,000 leagues per second).

---

8  "if you please" ("s.v.p." in the original)

It is fair to add that the light has devoted to its training every single moment since the first days of creation (which hasn't gotten any younger), while Terront has not yet practiced the bicycle for fifteen years.

Theoretically, Terront ought to make the trip around the world in seventy days. (You can shove it, my dear old Jules Verne!)

In practice, he ought to reduce it, the surface of the globe being appreciably more uneven than the slope of the Vélodrome in the Champs-de-Mars.

And, with these remarks, permit me, I beg you, to broadcast a desire that finds its echo in the heart of all 'recordmen'.[9]

Now that there are no more rollings, stagecoaches, mail wagons, the highways of France no longer have that lively animation which at one time rendered them so picturesque.

Even the highwaymen are extinct: Some, accustomed to the outdoors, practice the profession of pickpocket at the racetracks; the rest are devoted to high banking.

The more and more widespread practice of cycling, tends to return to our national highways their bustle of yesteryear.

Could the Gentlemen of the streets and bridges not apply, for the maintenance of the roads, processes better suited for bikes?

Stone, freshly broken, excellent for the the wheel of the truck or carriage, is worthless for the rubber of our machines, utterly worthless.

Ah! if I were the government!

*-translated by Olchar Lindsann*
from Alphonse Allais, *Le Parapluie de l'escouade*. 5th Ed. 1893. Paul Ollendorf: Paris.

~^~^~^~^~^~^~^~^~^~^~^~^~^~^~^~^~^~^~^~^~^~^~^~^~^~^~^~^~^~

# Two poems from *The Neuroses*, 1883
### *by Maurice Rollinat*

*The Decadent poet Maurice Rollinat was a close, long-time collaborator with Allais (above), first as members of the* **Hydropathes** *group, then in the* **Chat Noir.** *He published in the journal and performed at the cabaret, where he set his poems to music (as well as poems by Baudelaire) and sang them to his own piano accompaniment. "The Absinthe Drinker" describes a malady common to those who frequented the Chat Noir nightclub.*

9   English in the original.

# 1. Poor Little Absinthe Drinker

*(to Dr. Louis Julien)*

***Translator's Introduction:*** *Intoxicants have been with mankind since before recorded history. The knowledge of how to use them was, initially, the province of shamen, priests, herbalists, lone seekers and the like. With the advent of social structures (from tribes to cities) the context for taking intoxicants began to change. With the division of social time divided between labor and leisure, so too were intoxicants restricted to those few circumstances which were still sanctioned (religious rites, medical emergencies, etc.), so as not to interfere with productive 'labor time'.*

*But, like Pandora's Box, the use of intoxicants, though once known only to the elect few, became the province of the many, and this pharmacological knowledge could never be made obscure again. As societies became more and more complex, so increased the number of people who 'fell through the cracks' of those societies; the disenfranchised, the destitute, the mad…*

*To these unfortunates were left the means of escaping pain, fear, loneliness… albeit temporarily.*

*Intoxicants used as anodyne and panacea; a false hope and a cure as deadly as any disease. Pain delayed is still pain yet-to-come. True **Lethe** comes only for the dead, until then, there are only her pale, seductive and nefarious sisters: among which are **Opium** and **Absinthe**.*

She was always pregnant,
Or so it always seemed...
Poor little absinthe drinker!

She lived in fear
Of her brutal lover:
She was always pregnant.
On nights when the sky oozes,
She lay down beneath the open heavens.
Poor little absinthe drinker!

Those that debauchery exhausts
Leered at her with a bitter eye:
She was always pregnant!
In Paris, this labyrinth,
Immense as the sea,
Poor little absinthe drinker!

She went, dead-eyed,
Crawling along the walls like a worm...
She was always pregnant!

Oh! This faded skirt
Who dragged herself out every winter!
Poor little absinthe drinker!

Her voice was only a murmur,
In her stomach grew a cancer:
She was always pregnant!

What shy lament
Will speak its hideous statement!
Poor little absinthe drinker!

I see her, poor doe-eyed country-girl, again
As if it were yesterday:
She was always pregnant!

Frightened more and more
Of nothing at all, while turning her spoon;
Poor little absinthe drinker!

Once she'd had a pint
The coughing started, - oh! how she suffered,
She was always pregnant! -

She bitched: "This is destroying me!
I am already in Hell! "

Poor little absinthe drinker!

Nonetheless, she drank a pint
Of the awful green liquid:
She was always pregnant!

And Agony was painted
Upon her barely open eye;
Poor little absinthe drinker!

When her lover says, not kidding:
"You'll abort it, that's for damned sure!
"She was always pregnant."
　　　　—Poor little absinthe drinker!

*Translated by Raymond E. Andre III*

---

## 2. The Belovèd Embalmed
*À Joseph Carriès.*
*(Translation dedicated to Lady Shannon Valerian)*

So as to tear death from so beautiful an angel,
　　From the atrocious kisses of the worm,
I embalmed her in a strange box.
　　One winter's night:
From out of this frozen body, rigid and livid,
　　Came her poor dead organs,
And into this open stomach as bloody as it was empty
　　Were poured perfumed oils,

Chlorine, tar and powdered lime;
　　And when it was quite full,
A silver sewing needle passed through it
　　Making but a single crease upon her skin.

Her eyes where great Nature
      Had placed the azure of its skies
And which would have been devoured by pestilential decay,
      Were replaced by artificial blue eyes.

The pharmacist, with a certain gum,
      Succeeded in petrifying her;
And when he yapped, cheerfully, stinking of brandy:
      "That won't rot ever!"

I said to my dead love. "You would've been pierced like an old tree
      "By the reptiles of the tomb,
"Before the embalming: now, as hard as marble, Darling,
      "You won't lose the least shred!"

Then, alone, I painted her lips purple
      With essence of carmine,
I covered with jewels, rings and amulets
      Her slender neck and her frail hand.

I half-opened her eye-lids and closed her mouth
      Full of stupor and fright;
And, gravely, I placed her dainty slipper
      Upon her poor, small, cold foot.

I veiled the body in a gauze shroud,
      I unbound her long hair,
And falling upon my knees I passed from ecstasy
      To an atrocious and nervous delirium.

Then, in an intense neurotic paroxysm
      Crushing me like a weight of fatal lead,
Haggard, I spread upon her a long spray of roses
      Within her crystal bier.

The putrescent odors had escaped the room,
    And over golds and velvets
The breaths of benzoin, vetiver and amber
    Hovered hot, irritating and heavy.

And I gazed upon her, this precious mummy:
    And her beauty revived once more,
I dared to imagine that she was but lulled to sleep
    In the arms of pleasure.

And leading to a cool vault where balustrades
    Of black marble and massive gold,
Forever, gleam sepulchral lamps,
    Below a pensive skull,

The dead belovèd in her transparent and splendid coffin,
    Mocking putrefaction,
Sleeps, intact and serene, amorous and without guile,
    Before my astonished gaze.

*Translated by Raymond E. Andre III*

Both poems from Maurice Rollinat, *Les Névroses.* 1883. Charpentier: Paris.

~^~^~^~^~^~^~^~^~^~^~^~^~^~^~^~^~^~^~^~^~^~^~^~^~^~^~^~^~^~^~^~^~

**Manifest 2 & Manifest 3**    *by Edward Kulemin*

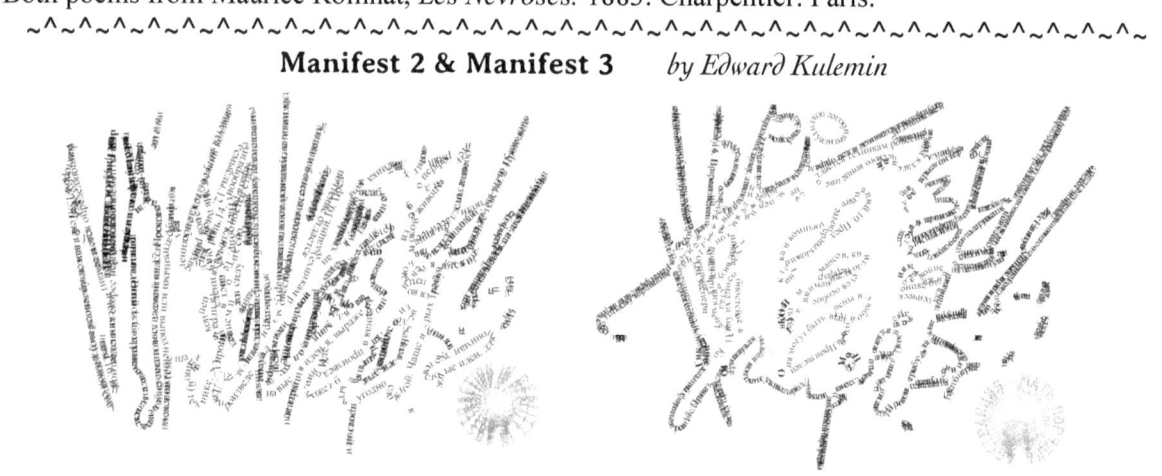

~^~^~^~^~^~^~^~^~^~^~^~^~^~^~^~^~^~^~^~^~^~^~^~^~^~^~^~^~^~^~^~^~^~^~

## Gothic Song (1849),
*by Gérard de Nerval*

*Nerval, was among the most influential of the first-generation avant-garde, though his poetry circulated only in journals and manuscript until long after his death. This decadent little poem was written for music by the frenetic composer Limnander for his opera Les Monténégrins in 1849. Gérard collaborated on the libretto with the Romanticist writer/historian Alboize Pujol.*

Lovely bride,
Your tears I praise!
The dew you've cried
Befits bouquets.

What's lovely knows
But once Spring's prime,
Let's sow the rose
The steps of Time!

Brunette or blonde,
Why choose just one?
For this world's God
Is known as Fun.

*Translated by Olchar E. Lindsann*

from Nerval, *Poesies*. Ed Mounir Hafez. 1964. Gallimard: Paris

## toutes les choses sont elles
### (1830/2016)
*by John M. Bennett, from CharlesNodier*

*Nodier's novel **Les Sept Chateaux du Roi de Bohême** (see next page) is strewn with list poems—inspired largely by Rabelais and Sterne—which have become staples in avant-garde writing ever since, from Gautier to the Surrealists to many threads of Otherstream writing. Bennett has broken apart, mixed up, and re-glued one such list in a posthumous collaboration.*

si tronquées mes pieds si mas
tiquées mes doigts my blood I
chewed si compliquées les
gommes I wrote you with
si déloquées les paroles
updown si imbriquées si ét
riquées yr short fat ton
ggues si détriquées my
burning shirts my sheets
my shits my shorts si dé
froquées si pelues si
trépelues si si farfelues my
farts com mand yr voices si
patraquées yr sleeps si
involues si goth iquées
que je me vois le dos
au miroir *la dos la pied la*
*doigt*

**D'après une liste de Charles Nodier,
dans Histoire du roi de Bohême, 1830**

37

~^~^~^~^~^~^~^~^~^~^~^~^~^~^~^~^~^~^~^~^~^~^~^~^~^~^~^~^~^~^~^~

# Invention (1830)
## by Charles Nodier

*Charles Nodier was a seminal figure in the founding of the avant-garde. His 1830 experimental novel* **The Seven Castles of the King of Bohemia** *contains not only this phonetic poem (built largely from onomatopoeia, of which he had compiled a dictionary), but also stunning visual, typographical, pictographic, and list-poems like the one used by Bennett in the previous piece. Nodier says: "...this page, entirely unique among all the written monuments of language, hides, beneath the appearance of a simple witticism, the strongest effort of creative imagination; the secret of the* **Novum organum**[10] *and the* **Characteristic***; the universal intelligence that the kantists, ecclesiastics and pundits, so in love with clarity, still seek gropingly!"*

Pif paf piaf patapan.

Ouhiyns ouhiyns.　　Ebrohé broha broha,　　Ouhiyns ouhiyns.

Hoé hu. Dia hurau. Tza tza tza.

Cla cla cla. Vli vlan. Flic flac. Flaflaflac.

Tza tza tza. Psi psi psi. Ouistle.

Zou lou lou. Rlurlurlu. Ouistle,

Cla cla cla. Flaflaflac.

Ta ta ta. Ta ta ta. Pouf.

Ouhiyns. Ebrohé broha. Ouhiyns ouhiyns.

Ta ta—ta ta—ta ta—ta ta—hup.

A u ho. Tza tza tza. O hem. O hup. O war!

Trrrrrrrrrrrrrrr. Hup. O hep. O hup. O hem. Hap!

Trrrrrrrrrrrrrrr. O hup. O hé. O halt! O! Oooooh!

Xi xi xi xi! Pic! Pan! Baoûnd.

Hourra!!!!!!!!

from Charles Nodier, *Les Sept Chateaux du roi de bohême / Les Quartre talismans.* 1852. *Lecou, Paris.*

~^~^~^~^~^~^~^~^~^~^~^~^~^~^~^~^~^~^~^~^~^~^~^~^~^~^~^~^~^~^~

---

10 Francis Bacon's book proposing a new form of logic.

*The Franco-American Symbolist Francis Vièle-Griffin, a close friend of Mallarmé and Jarry, wrote several poems in the recently-invented language of Volapük, a precursor of Esperanto. He was also among the first, in 1890, to predict the poetic use of manipulated sound in recorded poetry. The accent is always on the **last** syllable.*

## Volapük Fragments (1890)
*Toussaint-des-Mornes" (Francis Vièle-Griffin)*

> Alina das nëito, Mun,
> Desipol oba tikâli.
> Oblekôle kaladàli,
> Bludom del of a nedan vun.
>
> Polü nâta del fatela
> Cils ekômoms lôbo zi bed;
> Fukel omsik edlemom, yed
> Epukôms vips nâtadela.
>
> "Binols-od gudik, cils gâla,"
> Sagom bâledan," dat, füdo,
> Got omcs cils givom-la, do
> Man etos no melidom-la!

from *Entretiens politiques & littéraires*. Year 1, No. 1, April 1890. ed. Paul Adam & Francis Vièle-Griffin. Librairie de l'art indépendant: Paris.

~^~^~^~^~^~^~^~^~^~

*M.H. was born in Dallas in 1958. Shortly afterwards, fish fell from the sky.*

## Knife at Raintime (c.1980s)
*Michael Helsem*

> Fidil pefalöl dese lusil,
> O lecütel, tobuls no dönu
> olükömons is lienetiks.
> Exilonok mekavamüster
> nesinifodio sembal, e
> mutob gegivön ad ol voli
> kölöfikum keli älärnob
> da logs ola, voli de fil kel
> päfanon fa ob de oliks muds
> tel, e voli dolas luplikün
> in ola lad keli ädünob.

("Or fallen from the sorry sky, O great deceiver, Mad Octobers will not arrive here again. The artificial mystery has banished itself to some meaninglessness or other, & i must give you back the world more colorful i learned through your eyes, the world of fire that was caught by me from your mouths twain, & the world of most wolfish griefs in your heart which i served.")

~^~^~^~^~^~^~^~^~^~^~^~^~^~^~^~^~^~^~^~^~^~^~^~^~^~^~^~^~

The **Revenant Series** publishes translations, histories, and new editions of works related to the 19th Century avant-garde, including the Romanticist, Frenetic, Occultist, Utopian Socialist, Bohemian, Parnassian, Decadent, and Symbolist communities.

# New from mOnocle-Lash

***Pif Paf Patapan! A Sampler of Phonetic Poetry From the 19th Century***, *by Théophile Gautier, Charles Nodier, Paul Verlaine, & Francis Vielé-Griffin.* 8 pp. A pocket pre-history of sound poetry: five phonetic poems published between 1830 & 1891. The poets who were read by the Futurists, Dadas, & Zoumists, and whose experiments they consolidated into a new form.

***The Prelude: Translated into Even-More-Boring-and-Trite; Vol. 3,*** *by Fast Sedan Nellson & William Wordsworth.* 24 pp. The next thrilling, anxiously-awaited installment of Fast Sedan Nellson's masterpiece of translation, in which young Wordsworth *remains at school!*

# In Preparation for the mOnocle-Lash Revenants Series

***Some Squibs,*** *by Alphonse Allais.* Stories and poems by avant-satirist Allais (1854–1905): core member of the Hydropathes, Incoherents, and Chat Noir groups, painter of the first colour-field pictures, composer of the first soundless music score. *Tentative Winter 2016-17 release.*

***The Feminine Frenetic***, *ed. Olchar E. Lindsann.* A first sampling of poems by just a few of the dozens of female participants in the first self-declared "avant-garde" movement, Frenetic Romanticism, many of them unpublished in any language since 1836. A first step. *Tentative Spring 2017 release.*

***Philothée O'Neddy: Brigand of Thought.*** The first full-length collection in English of the Bouzingo co-founder, one of the most influential, yet forgotten, writers of the Romanticist avant-garde. Includes selections from his poetry, theory, fiction, criticism, & correspondence, memoirs by his friends and collaborators, plus a critical biography and bibliography, for the most comprehensive view of his total project ever published. *Tentative Summer 2017 release.*

Sept., A.Da. 100
A.H. 186
2016 C.E.

**mOnocle-Lash Anti-Press**
**REVENANT SERIES**
monoclelash.wordpress.com
monoclelash@gmail.com

# Rêvenance

## A Zine of Hauntings from Underground Histories

Issue No. 2                    August 2017 (A.Da. 101, A.H. 187)

## Featuring

**The Dead**: Marceline Desbordes-Valmore / Arthur Cravan / Célestin Nanteuil / The Chat Noir / Ivan Gilkin / Roger de Beauvoir / Fernand Clerget / Albert Sérieys / Francis Vielé-Griffin / "The German Princess" / Alphonse Karr / Charles-Henry Hirsch / Charles Whitehead / John Payne / Léon Gozlan

**The Living**: Olchar E. Lindsann / Gleb Kolomiets / Elizabeth Birdsall / Raymond E. André III

*Rêvenance* is dedicated to the forgotten or untold histories of 19th Century avant-garde and other countercultures. It promotes history practiced as game, as activism, as trans-generational collaboration, as communal memory, which runs athwart the academic, refuses to describe history as finished, which does not stand apart to observe its object from a distance, in the posture of false 'objectivity' which Power always assumes. Instead: a *committed* historiography, which does not stand outside the stream of time or apart from its object: intellectual and precise, yet ludic and multi-form, one moment manifest as an essay, the next as a poem. A historiography created *within* the utopian fringe, and for the same community, responsive to our changing conditions, needs, and desires. A historiography that *we take personally*, which merges imperceptibly into daily life, thought, and continued experimental practice and life.

The journal is closely integrated with the Revenant Archive of roughly 500 books, prints, manuscripts, and personal items from the 19th Century avant-garde, and much of the material is drawn from the archive's material. The journal explores forgotten and newly-discovered histories of avant-garde, radical activist, utopian, and other underground countercultures. While the primary focus is on the 19th Century, earlier and later material is also welcome, and contributions directly connecting counter-cultural movements and strategies across time are particularly encouraged. The primary goal is to explore histories, communities, and themes that are not consistently represented elsewhere. *Rêvenance* seeks to develop a community of independent DIY researchers who see historical work as part of a communal praxis directed toward contemporary and future change; it is a laboratory in which countercultural history is transmuted, reflected and disseminated in the current lifestyle, writing, music, art, and thought of present-day communities of dissent or otherness.

**Edited by Olchar E. Lindsann**
*Rights retained by translators & living writers*

All other texts in the public domain
Aug., A.Da. 101
A.H. 187
2017 A.D.

## mOnocle-Lash Anti-Press
monoclelash.wordpress.com
monoclelash@gmail.com

## Revenants Series
revenant-archive.blogspot.com
bouzingo.blogspot.com

# CONTENTS

*Many of the source texts are available online at gallica.bnf.fr and/or at archivc.org.*

**Cover image by Olchar E. Lindsann,** collaged from: Célestin Nanteuil, *Portrait of Roger de Beauvoir* (c.1840) & *De Profonds des amours* (c.1850), Merwart, *Editorial Breakfast at the Chat Noir* (1887), Jules Platier, *The Artistic Dandy* (1842), Baron & Nanteuil, Illustration for Fénelon's *Telemachus* (1840), and anonymous frontispiece to Joseph Bouchardy's *Paris the Bohemian* (1842). All constituent images are photocopied from original editions held in the Revenant Archive.

Send Submissions & Correspondence to monoclelash@gmail.com

*Olchar E. Lindsann is the editor of **Rêvenance** and **mOnocle-Lash Anti-Press**, a writer, cultural historian, organiser, and teacher. Current projects include research into 19th Century avant-garde phonetics, an anthology and biography of Bouzingo co-founder Philothée O'Neddy, chapbooks of Alphonse Allais, female French avant-gardists of the 1830s, and articles from Alphonse Karr's early DIY journal **Les Guêpes**. Kolomiets' essay appeared in Rêvenance 1.*

# pRe-face to Some Potential Histories
## In Response to Kolomiets' *What Governs the History of Art?*  (2017)
### *by Olchar E. Lindsann*

In the first issue of *Rêvenance*, Gleb Kolomiets spoke directly to the heart of this journal's goals in his call to, "reclaim historical narrative for personal needs or for needs of a community," identifying five structural "points of subjection" through which historical narrative and analysis tend to support state, corporate, and reactionary interests, and offering potential strategies to build what I have elsewhere called a radical historiography.[1] What is offered is the basis for a concerted and systematic exploration of what such a self-consciously *dynamic* and contrarian experience of communal history might become – not only within the cultural realm but for *all* socially, politically, and economically marginal communities – and this important venture elicits response.

For this reason, I intend here to respond with a few ideas that it provoked, and to preface my more long-term response to the essay through a series of related historical etudes. I invite further responses, and other potential systems; indeed, much of the material in R*êve-nance* could already be thought of in these terms. I will offer a few additional ideas as well, which might well be taken up for further exploration or application.

Kolomiets begins by warning us about the totalizing tendency of historical narrative,

---

1   Gleb Kolomiets, "What Governs the History of Art?" in *Rêvenance*, No. 1, Sept. 2016. mOnocle-Lash Anti-Press: Roanoke, VA, pp 6–8; and Olchar E. Lindsann, *Toward a Radical Historiography: Creative Sociality and the Traditions of Dissent*. 2011. Mycelium Samizdat Publishers: Decentralised. Both available online at the Internet Archive, archive.org

wherein, "the objects of historical narrative are in a subordinate position to the general rules of the organization of narrative and time." In addition to the strategies that he offers in response, the *archive* offers an existing model which (as the Rêvenant Archive attempts) can be radicalized as an historical model that is spatial and combinatory, ludic rather than linear and "necessary". Each element in an archive is a discrete unit, and their constituent artifacts (and the stories and contexts they carry with{in} them) can be organised simultaneously according to many different principles: chronological but also communal, bibliographic, linguistic, alphabetical, by provenance, origin, format, or even colour.

Another form with which some experimentation has begun is that of role-playing games, in which the "readers" of history inhabit the historical and psychological situations of the past. Since "actual" historical narrative and causality are suspended and (literally) open to play, historical emphasis is thrust upon *conditions*, rather than chronology, and problem-solving becomes the principle conduit of historical understanding. In this way, history is learned as a *strategic* faculty, and more directly applicable to present-day progressive practice. The role-playing game *Romantique*, set in the Paris cultural underground c.1830, is currently in development and play-testing and attempts to explore this possibility.[2]

Kolomiets warns in a footnote that subconscious conditioning remains an inevitable threat to any attempt to contest dominant structures. This threat might be met, and new positive strategies developed, by applying and adapting Surrealist and other psychoactivist methods to historiographic work. This area offers great potential for further development, to which the work of Lacan, Certeau, de Landa, and others provide glimpses. What would an oneirocritical history look like? A libidinal historiography? An automatic chronicle? How might chance procedures intervene in the research or analytical processes?

---

2   By Warren Fry and Olchar Lindsann. An earlier game set in 1920s Paris, *Zietgeist*, served as a prototype but has yet to see publication. Experiments in this area exist outside the avant-garde as well, cf. Paul Mason, "Culture Club: Role-Playing as a a means of experiencing different modes of thought," in *Interactive Fantasy: The Journal of Role-Playing and Story-making Systems*, No. 3, 1995.

To the five points of subjection identified by Kolomiets, I would offer a couple more. The first is *Communal Alienation* from history as both a presence and a process: both historical knowledge (presence) and especially research (agency) are too often relegated to specialists within a subculture, "contracted out" as it were, so that it fails to remain a living, active force in the community's continued life and development. Unless each of us is a historian in some small but engaged way, and shares that engagement with each other, our relationship to history and to time becomes passive. The linearity of conventional narrative can obscure the *continued* applicability and responsibility of history within the present and for the future, and weaken the contextual awareness and effectiveness of a subculture as a whole.

The second point of subjection, *Academic De-radicalization*, is related to the first. When those working and living within alternative traditions become alienated from their own histories, they cede the ground to academic scholars who, as avatars of Power, all too often manipulate our own narratives. They are either constructed so as to support that power (cf. Duchamp's readymades offered as antecedent for the commercialization of visual art via Pop, Conceptual Art, etc.) or to make our history itself disappear (cf. The slew of pre-Marxist socialist and proto-anarchist collectives, from the Athenaeum group to the Saint-Simonists to the Evadamists, who have been nearly forgotten even within radical culture). To combat both, we need historiographic work to become more widespread, more grass-roots, more personalized, in order to be decentralized, democratic and vital.

Another aspect I would add: in addition to historians, who continually renew and communicate with the past, we need *chroniclers* committed to communicating with the future: stewards of future histories. For models we might look to the Medieval chroniclers, the multi-volume French Romanticist anthologies of satirical chronicles of Parisian life, Decadent and Symbolist Roman-à-clefs, the Zurich "Dada Chronicle", and much of Jim Leftwich's recent activity.

All of the above may be expanded upon in the future by myself and (hopefully) others, but my first campaign shall take the form of six short, experimental historiographic test-cases to interrogate and build on the foundation of each of Kolomiets' five points of subjec-tion. These will be published over the course of Issues 3 – 8. The object of investigation in each essay will be chosen in accordance with the historiographic principle to explored; some will deal with better-known avant-history such as Dada, some with history already fallen prey to the master narrative, such as the avant-Romanticism, with over-lap between essays in order to see how different approaches yield different views of the same "topics". These will be thought-experiments, not in-depth studies, and will rely primarily upon my on-hand knowl-edge applied to the model in question; the word *essay*, after all, is rooted in the *attempt*. Their aim will be to suggest further avenues of study and to instigate and refine new historical methods, awarenesses, and strategies. They constitute a *next* step, not a final step:

1. ***Temporal Organisation.***[3] A cyclical narrative telling the story of several riots, includ-ing those at the premiers of *The Burgraves*, *The Gas Heart*, *Hernani*, *Hurlements en favour de Sade*, *The Rite of Spring*, *Tannhauser*, and two different productions of *Ubu Roi*.

2. ***Composition of Narrative.***[4] A heroic-investigative poem on the 1830 Battle of *Hernani*.

3. ***Totalization***. A triplicate list of as many people as possible who participated in some way in the Dada movement–in any journal, exhibition, manifesto, performance, col-laboration, or demonstration. One version will be organised by Name, one by Medi-um, and one by Locality, with redundancies where appropriate. No other narrative or

---

3  Works which have begun to address this point of subjection include Greil Marcus's *Lipstick Traces* and my *The Ecstatic Nerve*.

4  This point of subjection has begun to be addressed by Ed Sanders' Investigative Poetics, Banville's historical poems on the Romanticist movement, Hans Richter's personal approach to *Dada: Art and Anti-Art* and Huelsenbeck's *Tales of a Dada Drummer*, not to mention Ball's mythologized history of Zurich Dada in *Tenderenda the Fantist*, Gautier and O'Neddy among other Romanticists in their poetic and quasi-fictional self-representations, Vaneigem's *Cavalier History of Surrealism*, Lamborn Wilson's work on Pirate Utopias, and the various histories/chronicles/fictions of the Neoist Apart-ment Festivals. The predominance of the first person in the essay that *you*, my dear reader, are cur-rently perusing can be looked at in the same light.

hierarchy will be interposed. (This may be published last, due to the amount of leg-work required.)

4. *Causal Relationships.* Kolomiets' caution against promoting, "a genealogy of styles," and of a, "rigid conceptual structure with the powerful relationships of subordination" are well-taken, and I shall experiment in this essay with applying Dada and Surrealist techniques to historical research and analysis. I would argue, nonetheless, that once toppled from its hegemonic position by means of the strategies suggested here and others, causality still has a role to play. As implied above when discussing role-playing, it is necessary for the development of the strategic capacity necessary for the continued survival of inherently tenuous communities; however, it must be vigilant against forming master-narratives, subjecting the specific event to general or abstract systemification, or promoting an instrumentalist conception of the historical process.

5. *Context.* Two routes to addressing this issue are suggested, so my response will be two-fold: an essay on the communal spaces (contexts) of the Jeunes-France/Bouzin-go group, over-saturated with contextual notes, as per my usual practice; and an under-saturated essay on a Post-NeoAbsurdist event, giving minimal context outside that community's specific micro-history. In an anglophone context, the idea of mini-mizing context can raise spectres of the hyper-alienated, a-historical and amoral stance of the New Criticism; my attempt here will be to eliminate the context *of* the event's social dynamic, without eliminating the social dimension of the event itself, avoiding formal elements as the parameters of isolation.

These essays done, something, at least, should have been stirred up – and if any historical cadavers are dislodged by our prodding and float to the surface, they can be revivified, how-ever grotesque or unexpected the result, in *Rêvenance.*

~^~^~^~^~^~^~^~^~^~^~^~^~^~^~^~^~^~^~^~^~^~^~^~^~^~^~^~^~^~^~

*This unsigned article, attributed to Léon Gozlan, contains one of the earliest satires of the avant-garde, from the government-owned satirical magazine* Figaro, *which would ironically publish Marinetti's* Fascist Futurist Manifesto *nearly 80 years later. As with many of the pieces in this journal, the translation process is fundamentally communal, and in this case was undertaken by specific request from within the Victor Hugo fandom community. The conversations arising from and around the translation have been included in the footnotes.*

*Translator's Introduction: The bousingots, or bouzingos, were a particularly rowdy and politically radical subculture of early 1830s French Romanticism. For the Les Mis fans, it may be of interest to note that one of their leaders was Petrus Borel, whom Hugo fictionalized a few decades later as Bahorel, and who was famous among his peers for republican opinions and scarlet waistcoats. I don't know if he's the one specifically being satirized here, or if it's aimed at the whole crowd equally, but it seems very possible that Borel was a specific inspiration.*

# The Red Bousingot   (1832)

## *by Léon Gozlan*

The bousingot is inexhaustible, he will leave his mark like the *camaraderie*, the *piqueurs* and the *jeunes-frances*.[5] If one were still writing books, one would put him in the books; if one still had theaters, one would drag him over the theaters by his beard and by his hat. The bousingot belongs to painting, statuary, to trestle-stages,[6] to the Cockaigne pole,[7] to Chinese

---

5  According to my Local Romanticism Expert (hi @pilferingapples), the camaderie, the piqueurs, and the jeunes-frances were all the same group as the bouzingos/bousingots. The ~~Jeune-Frances~~ Jeunes-France (oops, thanks also to Pilf for correcting my spelling) was another term for the bouzingos, coined by this magazine and then adopted with a mocking misspelling by the group. Camaraderie, i.e. friendship, was one of their sacred ideals, and dramatic odes to friends and friendship abounded. I don't know where "piqueurs" comes from, but it's a term that means (among other things) "thieves," so I assume it was more thumbing of their noses at society by mockingly presenting themselves as dangerous rulebreakers. [Lindsann note: Yep, Philothée O'Neddy confirmed as much in an 1862 open letter.]

6  "Trestle-stages": the word tréteaux seems to mean either trestles (like, sawhorses) or a stage set upon them, especially at a fair or other temporary popular event, if I'm understanding my dictionaries right.

7  The Cockaigne pole ("le mât de Cocagne") is a large greased or soaped pole planted in the ground, like a flagpole or mast, which people try to climb to get at a prize at the top. It's a tradition for at least some festivals, apparently! (Here's a brief mention of it in the English wikipedia, and a longer

Bousingots

shadows, to blockades at the intersection, he's the sea-foam of politics,[8] the flower of the ridiculous, the prototype of all exaggeration. By nature he's a being of 93 in politics, honorably refined for his fashion, a royal bird for his habits. We're waiting for Poulaine slippers.[9]

After having worn out the patent leather hat and the large blue ribbon, he's just adopted the red hat. The bousingot wears the red hat; add on a hanging cord and two knots and the bousingot will be a cardinal. He was a sailor with patent leather, he'll be a cardinal with the red hat.

A general rule for foreigners. Green men with epaulettes and a gold baldric aren't colonels, they're hunters; they carve at the table; black men, all black, with ragged coats, and strong soft boots clasping up to mid-thigh, aren't poets or whalers, they're undertakers; men who have red hats, a blue ribbon, and who would be tricolors if they had a white face and linens, are bousingots. The little cafés are overflowing with them, the Pont-Neuf is groaning with them, Sainte-Pélagie has them to spare,[10] the faubourg St-Germain abounds with them.

one in the French wikipedia.)

8  "The sea-foam of politics": the French is "l'écume de la politique," which as far as I can tell either means the froth on the surface, or a more pejorative "the scum/dregs of politics." Since the rest of this is ridiculing their fashion, I went with the more superficial option, but it might instead be meant as a deeper insult.

9  Poulaine slippers (souliers à la Poulaine), also called crakows or crackowes in English, are those medieval shoes with the really long pointy toes. (English wikipedia, French wikipedia.)

10  ~~"Sold out of them"~~ later edit: @robertawickham suggested "has them to spare," which I think is better. There's a splotch over the first letter of "_evendre," and "revendre" was my only guess. ~~Even~~

A month ago, you could have seen them in black varnish; it's too late, they're red: the heat has colored them like lobsters, crabs and crayfish. They're not harmful.

Hurry to go and see them, be glad to encounter them, because soon, maybe tomorrow, they'll have green hats like the penniless of old times, or blue hats, like leprechauns of the time when there were leprechauns, or the hats of free men, which is to say no hats.

Hurry, because they're still walking on their feet, they're breathing with their noses, even if the nose is right in the center; we're assured that they eat; it was confirmed to me that they think sometimes.

You might well find them walking in carts, with gloves on their feet, slippers on their hands, if you catch them too late.

Why did they pick red? It's because red is the color of blood, blood which is their color, their principles; it's because red is fire, the color of conflagration, conflagration which is their color; it's because red is the color of anger, anger which is their color; it's because red is the color of one of the three furies of mythology, furies which are their color; it's because red makes itself with firewood, like wine. That's why they adopted the red hat.

Fathers and mothers, whom I honor, if you ask what your sons are doing in Paris, if they're keeping busy, if they're reading, if they're studying, we answer you in the way of newspapers, that they have the red hat, the blue ribbon, the yellow linen.[11]

Once there was only one man in France who wore a red hat; it was the hangman; he had the right to have a red coat too: that'll come.[12]

*Translated by Elizabeth Birdsall*

from *Figaro*. Year 7, No. 83 (March 23, 1832). Sole Edition: Paris. from the Revenant Archive.

~~with that I'm not totally sure I'm translating "Sainte-Pélagie en a à revendre" quite correctly.~~

11 It's entirely possible that yellow linens were a fashion I just don't know about. My guess, however, is that the mention of "yellow linens" at the end is meant as a cheap shot about bousingot students not doing their laundry often enough and just slumming around in stained shirts.

12 [the original footnote here contained a notification to several interested members of the fandom community that this translation had been posted]

~^~^~^~^~^~^~^~^~^~^~^~^~^~^~^~^~^~^~^~^~^~^~^~^~^~^~^~^~

*Marceline Desbordes-Valmore exercised a multidisciplinary influence on French Romanticism as writer and actress and opera singer. Her formally innovative, self-searching work laid much of the goundwork for the movement's lyric verse, and its often fervent and dark nature exercgted an important influence on the later avant-garde, including Baudelaire, the Parnassians, Verlaine (who included her in his Decadent anthology of* Damned Poets*), and Jarry, who has Faustroll include her posthumous children's story 'Le Serment des petits hommes' (The Little Men's Prom - ise) in his indispensable 'Livres pairs' to accompany his voyage. The following poem, with its curiously haunting rhythm, was found by the Romanticist critic Saint-Beuve among her papers after her death.*

## The Parted (published 1860)

### *by Marceline Desbordes-Valmore*

Do not write. I am sad, and wish my life were over.
The fair spring without you? — Oh, night of lightless gloom! —
I fold my idle arms which cannot clasp thee more —
To knock at my heart's door, like knocking on a tomb.
Do not write!

Do not write. We learn only from ourselves to die.
Do not query God . . . but yourself, if I love you!
From the depth of your lack to hear your loving cry,
Is to listen to the spheres without mounting thereunto.
Do not write.

Do not write. I dread you; I fear the things I think;
My mind clings to your voice which has so often called.
Do not show living water to one who cannot drink.
A true portraiture is a note fondly scrawled.
Do not write!

Do not write those soft words I don't dare read within:
It seems as if your voice scatters them on my heart;
As if I see them blazing across your grin;
It seems as if a kiss imprints them on my heart.
Do not write!

*-translated by Olchar E. Lindsann*
*& John Payne*

from Marceline Desbordes-Valmore, *Poésies inédits.* 1860. Jules Fick: Geneva.

~^~^~^~^~^~^~^~^~^~^~^~^~^~^~^~^~^~^~^~

*Roger de Beauvoir was best-known in his day for his idiosyncratic Dandyism, who served as inspiration for Charles Baudelaire, Barbey d'Aurevilly, and others. He was also a founder of the avant-garde Bohême Doyenné in the late 1830s and early '40s, an amalgam of ex-members of the Jeunes-France, radical dandies, and young Romantics. Despite his frivolous reputation (like many dandies, he dressed himself into poverty), his social conscience was strong, as seen in the unapologetic attack on his own white race in the following text, which introduced the first book about this 18th Century ex-slave who became a respected composer and commander in the French Revolution. The father of Beauvoir's friend Alexandre Dumas had also been born into slavery, and served under the Chevalier in an all-black regiment.*

**Roger de Beauvoir**, *c. 1840, by the Bouzingo co-founder Célestin Nanteuil. from the Revenant Archive.*

# from **Forward to *The Chevalier de Saint-George*** (1840)
*by Roger de Beauvoir*

## To the Duke
## of Fitz-James[13]

My dear Duke,

There are books that one composes with one's friends in mind; the one you are about to read is of their number.

In writing the history of the *Chevalier de Saint-Georges*, I often evoked in my thoughts your noble father, who himself passed brilliantly through this eighteenth century, whose thousand hues are reflected by my protagonists.

---

13 The sponsor of the project.

53

*In the book's unsigned frontispiece, the Chevalier de Saint-George is portrayed as extremely light-skinned.*

Better than myself – beyond all doubt – to the aid of my warm and inspired discourse, he must have maintained in the reader's heart some love and some pity for this century, all of whose glories we are unanimous in insulting and which we deck out as we please in a mantle of vices, without imagining that for most of these men these vices, which were imposed upon them by their epoch, were at least redeemed by elegance and spirit.

The eighteenth century, that honest child that the Philosophes lost, shall always be an under-appreciated century as long as one separates the *Encyclopédie* from its corruption and England from its faults.[14] We must take on this century not only as an event, but as a question.

A profound question in fact, my dear Duke, which is to know by what unlikely train of events and associations such an epoch, in falling, dragged everything along with it in its drop: everything, from respect for royalty to respect for property, for the same hammer-blow which struck the throne reduced the colonial system to rubble. See this countryside where every social principle is beaten into submission, where the history of ideas becomes as bizarre as that of mankind! There, each the tournament warrior enters the arena with his colours and armour; we recognise them, we denominate them: Voltaire, Franklin, Mirabeau streak across these times like speeding meteors. Around them are grouped paradox and truth, ignorance and knowledge; the camps are formed, they thrash, they speak, they dispute, as to whom shall be king! Never have we seen such a movement and such tumult; the army of rhetoricians swarmed in everywhere, the most mediocre receives the watchword,

---

14 I have retained the French orthography in both words to emphasise the historical specificity of Beauvoir's references to the Revolutionary project of the French Enlightenment polymaths, lost by rendering the simple English Philosophers and Encyclopedia.

obeys Diderot while waiting for them to obey Marat.[15] As the pamphlets were more than ever the order of the day, it is difficult to form a precise idea of men; they exalt them to the skies, or drag them in the sewer. More than once, and when the lava should have cooled, what text for the writer, what unstoppable curiosity to traverse this immense battlefield and to recognise each of these dead faces! If it must be confessed to you, my dear Duke, I only accept such a perilous mission with a shudder. At each shroud that I have lifted up in order to examine the men who once rubbed shoulders with the heroes of this book, my heart pounded, I was afraid. When I found myself face to face with Philippe-Equality, there alone did I regain my breath and courage . . . . . that one is excessively judged, is that not true?

After these scattered comments, you can already see for yourself, my dear Duke, that this book should be at same time a story of a man, and of an idea; that idea is this:

Prior 1492, there was an opinion which did not exist, or which at any rate impacted nobody in the social order; since that epoch, it has spread into two worlds, and today it has taken refuge in one alone.

This opinion merits study.

In 1492, Christopher Columbus conquers the New-World.

By 1592, the primitive population of a great part of the New-World is exterminated by the whites.

By 1692, the whites resolve to transport blacks into these very countries in which they have exterminated the population. Louis XIV published the Code for Blacks. This race is thrown in with beasts of burden, the jew himself is less oppressed.

Thus it is posited in principle that the black or colored man is deprived of the gift of intelligence.

The 18th Century, that great arsenal against prejudices, attacks this opinion.

In 1798, the blacks massacre the whites in Saint-Domingue. Three negroes, Toussaint-l'Ouverture, Dessalines et Rigaud, compete for some time, not only against the politics, but also the armies of France, Spain, and England.

Since then—in more than one country—and especially in France, men of color

---

15 *les plus indifférens reçoivent le mot d'ordre, et l'on obéit à Diderot en attendant que l'on obéisse à Marat.*

proved that they did not wish to remain strangers either to political struggles, nor to those of the mind.

Nonetheless the prejudice is still all-powerful in America!

. . . . . . . . . . . . . . . . . . . . . . . . . . . . . . . . . . . . . . . . . . . . . .

I only put forth this idea here as a fact; only the story evolved from that fact is intimately linked to that of the man whose strange figure appears perpetually in these pages.

This man, the Chevalier de Saint-Georges, the brilliant mulatto, the man of attacks, of good luck and feasts; unique man, indeed, whose skeleton a propitious chance made me discover, on which still hangs a Tonkin sword, decorated with a beautiful knot of silver.

Should it appear frivolous, at first glance, the life of such a man, I dare promise, dear Duke, that it contains adventures of a drama intimate enough to arouse your attention. Saint-Georges set foot in turn upon two craters, that of Saint-Domingue and that of Paris; in both revolution seethed. Misrepresented by jealous slander, the life of this *black Don Juan*, as he was dubbed by his contemporaries, must have come to resent the effect of certain intimate perils which the loyalty and nobility of his soul rejected. The first line[16] portrays that of a prince who only called himself his benefactor in order to exploit him to his profit. The second section of the book returns upon this prince the disgrace of this odious calculation. I should add that only by force of care and studious searches have I managed, dear Duke, to discover in this man the distinctive features and traits which contribute as much to the history of the eighteenth century as his do. Oral tradition, which is to say informal conversation with various living remainders from his day, kindly storytellers who have leafed on my behalf through the archives of their memory, has better repaid my efforts than the dry skin of biographies and [bibliographic] notices, all inept, contradictory or truncated.[17]

---

16 Untranslatable pun with what is in English the "front line" in a military sense.

17 ***Beauvoir's Note***: We do not pretend that we make ourselves exclusive biographer; far from it! and we count on using more than once the privilege granted to novelists. But for promised biographies it's another thing, and he admits to making them put their finger on their blunders.
The Universal Biography says, in the article 'Saint-Georges', that he enrolled in the musketeers some time after his arrival in Paris. Here is one erroneous fact. For to be simply an officer in the army, he had to prove nobility, all the more so for a body as privileged as the musketeers.

To contest the immense successes of the Chevalier de Saint-Georges, his grace, his radiance, would be to deny the popularity of his name.

*Translated by Olchar E. Lindsann*

from Roger de Beauvoir, *Le Chavalier de Saint-Georges.* 1840. 2nd Ed.. Bibliothèque Choisie, H.-L. Delloye, Paris. Vol. 1.                    from the collection of the Revenant Archive.

~^~^~^~^~^~^~^~^~^~^~^~^~^~^~^~^~^~^~^~^~^~^~^~^~^~^~^~^~^~

*A historiography of the oppressed will always be, in part, a historiography of crime. Since time immemorial, those who have felt disenfranchised from their dominant culture have enjoyed tales of outlaws, robbers, pirates, and other criminals outwitting the avatars of power; examples include the cunning thievery of Odysseus, the voyages of Sinbad, the adventures of Robin Hood, the exploits of privateers and pirates, Billy the Kid, Bonnie and Clyde, gangster rap, and on and on. The following text is drawn from an anthology of biographies of famous British outlaws, complete with the rather rough wood-cuts that adorned the ephemeral press of the day. Presented simply as a rollicking (yet cautionary) yarn about a master scam artist, it in fact portrays a woman who turned every stereotype, hypocrisy, social convention, and misogynist habit that she encountered against her "victims" – all of them predatory wealthy men. A pencil annotation on the copy in the Revenant Archive attributes the anonymous text to Charles Whitehead.*

## The German Princess (1836)

*by Charles Whitehead (Published Anonymously)*

Though this remarkable female character was denominated a German Princess, for a reason which will be mentioned in the course of her narrative, she was a native of Canterbury, and her father a chorister of that cathedral. From her sprightly and volatile disposition,

---

One finds with astonishment in this selfsame Universal Biography that Saint-Georges would have been named captain of the guard of the Duke of Chartres (also known as Philippe-Equality). He must in truth have had no such idea at that period to advance such a supposition, given that to be captain of the guard of a prince of the blood, one had to prove nobility dating from the year 1399, according to the statutes; to have been presented at Versailles and to have obtained the agreement of the king to exercise this duty near a prince of the royal blood. It is captain of the hunt that the Bibliography should say. Saint-Georges owed in fact this place to Madame de Montesson.

she at an early period took delight in reading the novels that were at that time fashionable, —such as *Parismus and Parismanus*, *Don Bellianis of Greece*, *Amadis de Gaul*, and *Cassandra* and *Cleopatra* ; and in a little time really believed what she wished, even that she was a princess.

But in her marriage she lost sight of her exalted conceptions, and united her fortune with a journeyman shoemaker. She resided with him until she had two children, who both died in their infancy. The industrious shoemaker was unable to support her extravagance, so that she at last left him, to seek her fortune elsewhere.

A woman of her figure, beauty, and address, was not long before she procured another husband. She went to Dover, and married a surgeon of that place, but, being apprehended and tried at Maidstone for having two husbands, by some dexterous manoeuvre she was acquitted.

✻    ✻    ✻

*[She goes to Europe, grafts money off of a few wealthy vacationers, and returns to England in the guise of a disinherited German 'Princess']*

✻    ✻    ✻

She landed at Billingsgate, one morning very early in the end of March 1663, and found no house open until she came to the Exchange inn, where she attained to the dignity of a German princess in the following manner. In this inn, she got into the company of some gentlemen who, she perceived, were full of money, and these addressing her in a rude manner, she began to weep most bitterly, exclaiming that it was extremely hard for her to be reduced to this extreme distress, who was once a princess. Here she recited the story of her extraction and education, and much about her pretended father, the lord Henry Vanwolway, a prince of the empire, and independent of every man but his Imperial Majesty. M Certainly," said she, " any gentleman here present may conceive what a painful situation this must be to me to be thus reduced, brought up as 1 have been under the care of an indulgent father, and in all the luxuries of a court. But, alas! what do I say? — Indulgent father! was it not his cruelty which banished me, his only daughter, from his dominions, merely for marrying, without his knowledge, -a nobleman of the court whom I loved to excess? Was it not my fa '-her who occasioned my dear lord and husband to be cut off in the bloom of his age, by falsely accusing him of a design against his person, — a deed which his virtuous soul abhorred ?" Here she pretended that the poignancy of her feelings would allow her to relate no more of her unfortunate history.

The whole company was touched with compassion at the melancholy tale, which she related with so much unaffected simplicity, that they had not a doubt of its truth. Compassionating her unfortunate situation,
they requested her acceptance of all the money they had about them, promising to return again with more. They were as good as their promise, and she ever after went by the name of the unfortunate German Princess.

❊     ❊     ❊

She was then introduced as an actress among the players, and by them supported for some time. Upon the strength of her popularity the house was often crowded, and the public curiosity was excited by, a woman who had made such a figure in the world, and was receiving great applause in her dramatic capacity. She generally appeared in characters suited to her habits of life, and those scenes which had been rendered familiar to her by former deception and intrigues. But what tended chiefly to promote her fame, was a play called the "German Princess," written principally upon her account, in which she spoke the following prologue in such a manner as gained universal applause.

> I've passed one trial, but it is my fear
> I shall receive a rigid sentence here :
> You think me a bold cheat, but case 't were so,
> "Which of you are not ? Now you 'd swear, I know ;
> But do not, lest that you deserve to be

Censured worse than you can censure me ;
The world 's a cheat, and we that move in it
In our degrees do exercise our wit;
And better 't is to get a glorious name,
However got, than live by common fame.

The Princess had too much mercury in her constitution to remain long within the bounds of a theatre, when London itself was too limited for her volatile disposition. She did not, however, leave the theatre until she had procured many admirers. Her history was well known, as well as her accomplishments and her gallantry, and introduced her into company. She was easy of access, but in society carried herself with an affected air of indifference.

❊     ❊     ❊

[*A string of liaisons, following a similar pattern, ensues.*]

❊     ❊     ❊

Her numerous and varied adventures would far exceed the limits appropriated to one life in this volume. It is sufficient to observe, that rather than her hands should be unemployed, or her avaricious disposition unsatisfied, she would carry off the most trifling article ; that, according to the proverb, all was fish that came into her net; and that when a watch, a diamond, or piece of plate could not be found, a napkin, a pair of sheets, or any article of wearing apparel, would suffice.

from Anonymous [Charles Whitehead], *Lives and Exploits of the Most Noted Highwaymen, Robbers and Murderers, of All Nations, Drawn From the Most Authentic Sources and Brought Down to the Present Time.* (Undated, c. 1850) Silas Andrus & Son: Hartford.
    from the collection of the Revenant Archive.

~^~^~^~^~^~^~^~^~^~^~^~^~^~^~^~^~^~^~^~^~^~^~^~^~^~^~^~^~^~^~^~^~

~^~^~^~^~^~^~^~^~^~^~^~^~^~^~^~^~^~^~^~^~^~^~^~^~^~^~^~^~^~^~^~

[illustration: people gathered around a cabaret table with a waiter, dog, and newspapers]

EDITORIAL BREAKFAST AT THE CHAT NOIR.

*Editorial Breakfast at the Chat Noir*, 1887. by [David?] Merwart. *The **Chat Noir** cabaret was one of the few real mixing-grounds of avant-garde subculture with mainstream popular culture in the late 19th Century, becoming famous for its riotous combination of riotous dance, experimental comedy, both cutting-edge and dance hall music, avant-garde poetry, and its eclectic clientele of Bohemian students and artists, urban workers, Symbolist writers, absinthe-addicts, society dilettantes, sex-workers, and eventually curious tourists.*

*Soon it launched its own journal, which became both a weekly document of the micro-community who met regularly at the cabaret and an influential magazine of avant-garde humour with a readership of 20,000. Though the masthead lists Rodolphe Salis and Alphonse Allais as editors, writing and editing the journal was a collective effort, usually done in the cabaret itself in informal conditions, as shown in this etching from Harpers. It also lists Maurice Isabey as "Administrator" and two "secretaries of direction": a rotating cast of Chat Noir habitués, plus occasional fleeting editorial positions such as "Musician of the Future," held by Donizetti in December 1889 and "Always forgotten," held by Chapsal the same month. Its playful, self-referential communal nature resonates strongly with many later avant journals such as* Fuck You: A Magazine of the Arts *,* The Lost and Found Times*, and the* in-Appropriated Press.

from *Harper's New Monthly Magazine.* Vol. 78, Dec. 1888–May, 1889. Harpers: New York.

*Fernand Clerget and Albert Sérieys were among the more elusive writers of the Chat Noir group, despite having published regularly in the journal. The group delighted in sound-play and often seem to compete for the most outré rhyme schemes around which to spin their verses, usually to very funny ends. This reflects the Chat Noir's musical orientation, and many of these poems were performed to music.*

*Clerget's 'Ballad of the Poor Rhymers' uses only two rhyme terminations in 28 lines, five of which are answered by the word* sommes, *and another by* assomes. *It may well be the result of a writing game or challenge, for Albert Sérieys' poem, published on the same day directly beside it, also plays heavily on the same terminal vowel, and also rhymes* sommes *with itself. The most appropriate way to render both poems' virtuoso sound-work and lurching, insistent rhythm seemed to be through a ludic transduction of their sound.*

## Balled at napalm air-Rimmers

### *by Fernand Clerget* (1889)

Chewy fremen sat butresses
Ochre ants and savior the psalms;
Churching pours liquor eros is,
Sand river delights our new psalms,
The bell it toils all blue psalms
Cleans us all mason no clambers;
Rich desperate, leggers of psalms,
Who saw vaunt napalm air-Rimmers?

March and debut in scent asses,
Talkey suit on our noose is psalms:
The gist is you'd hiss us passes;
Prince of preen, t'wacky psalms
Tests who jaded train ail her psalms,
A toy, Volley, key desk humours:
Too sure, too sure maim fat homes!…
Who saw vaunt napalm air-Rimmers?

## Ballade des Pauvres Rimeurs

### *by Fernand Clerget* (1889)

Fuyant chemins et buts tracés
Où courent sans savoir les hommes;
Cherchant pour leurs corps harassés,
Sans rêver des lits où nous sommes,
La belle étoile et les beaux sommes
Qui ne sont mais en nos clameurs;
Riches d'esprit, légers de sommes,
Où s'en vont les pauvre Rimeurs?

Marchand de butins entassés,
Toi qui sous ton or nous assomes:
Légiste issu des us passés;
Prince suprême, toi qui sommes
Tes sujets de traîner leurs sommes,
Et toi, Valet, qui dessous meurs:
Toujours, toujours mêmes fantômes!…
Où s'en vont les pauvres Rimeurs?

| | |
|---|---|
| Any less chumps, the boys glassy, | Emmi les champs, les bois glacés, |
| A semester days atoms | En ces mystères des atomes |
| Keats only corpse in lacy, | Qui tiennent les corps enlacés, |
| Saw vaunt chaw talk elk ever toms | S'en vont, chantant quelques vieux tomes |
| Daring door-key solid bombs | De rimes d'or qui sont les baumes |
| They know saturn well rumours, | De nos éternelles rumeurs, |
| As you float perfect dollar palms: | Et soufflant parfois dans leurs paumes: |
| Who saw vaunt napalm air-Rimmers? | Où s'en vont les pauvres Rimeurs? |

### INVOICE

Prince, March on, queso vote-domes
Rally language they say moors,
Near hay jam hay acid and Gnomes
Who saw vaunt napalm air-Rimmers.

### ENVOI

Prince, Marchand, qui sous vos dômes
Raillez l'angoisse des semeurs,
N'irez jamais au cie des Nomes
Où s'en vont les pauvres Rimeurs.

---

## Mellow Tea (1889)

*by Albert Sérieys*

*a Friend o' my Sod*

The man to the grass me wave
Man plunger lit tundra law,
Salve Rabelais I'm a slave
Llama sabre meal trip fall.

The man seeps launch along draw
If you say, the man stalk a lean,
My font sunday, gondola fawn,
A luscious son demand o' lean.

## Mélodie (1889)

*by Albert Sérieys*

*à Fernand Mazade*

Les mains dont les grâces mièvres
M'infligèrent leurs tendres lois,
Savent rapeller à mes lèvres
Les baisers permis d'autrefois.

Les mains si blanche aux longs doigts
Effusés, les mains tant câlines,
Me font songer, quand je les vois,
A la chanson des mandolines.

| | |
|---|---|
| The man lily hell a bean, | Les main liliales et fines |
| To prove crouton taper done, | D'où peuvent choir tant de pardons, |
| Aw, sue the pudding marine, | Ont, sous les pudiques malines, |
| Diaper nest who abbot one. | De pernicieux abandons. |
| | |
| Of thaw diskette new pear done | En foi de ce que nous pardons |
| – Oh! lament yucky new psalms! – | – Oh! les mendiants que nous sommes! – |
| Cat'd do bombs edit ton | Que de doux baumes et de dons |
| Serin delicate gnomes! | Se rendent-elles économes! |
| | |
| Parlay you live to barley psalms, | Pour les yeux la de voir les hommes, |
| The man can deed Oprah me | Les mains candides ont promis |
| Along, awesome peppermill psalms, | Aux longs, aux sempiternels sommes, |
| Learned warplane tiffs, learned what saw me; | Leurs doigts plaintifs, leurs doigts amis; |
| | |
| A new new under me | Et nous nous endormis |
| Sue learn muse he call nap rose, | Sous leurs musicales névroses, |
| Rest spectre, whom blah, sue me, | Respectueux, humbles, soumis, |
| Deplore and no pope peers close . . . | Des pleurs en nos paupières closes . . . |

*-transliterated by Olchar E. Lindsann*

from *Chat Noir*, No. 404. Oct. 12, 1889. Ed. Rodolphe Salis & Alphonse Allais. Paris.
from the collection of the Revenant Archive.

~^~^~^~^~^~^~^~^~^~^~^~^~^~^~^~^~^~^~^~^~^~^~^~^~^~^~^~^~^~

## Found Text Reported in Les Guêpes (1840)
*by Alphonse Karr*

We read in a journal: "They found in the river the corpse of a soldier sliced into bits and stitched into a sack . . . *which fact excludes any suspicion of suicide.*"

*-Translated by Olchar Lindsann.*

from *Les Guêpes*, Jan., 1840. Ed. & Written by Alphonse Karr. Self-Published, Paris.
from the Revenant Archive

~^~^~^~^~^~^~^~^~^~^~^~^~^~^~^~^~^~^~^~^~^~^~^~^~^~^~^~^~^~

*Gleb Kolomiets is extremely active in the contemporary Russian avant-garde, as writer, theorist, publisher, translator, organiser, curator, and historian. He is the editor of the journal* **Slova***, an important point of international exchange among radical, anti-commercial creative workers; founder of the decentralized underground press* **Mycelium***; and has organised many cultural events in Smolensk and elsewhere, including the* **First Russian Asemic Exhibit***.*

## How to Find the Historical Unconscious? (2017)

### *by Gleb Kolomiets*

Revolutions often give birth to totalitarian regimes. These are cases in which events and social movements, declaring their goals as emancipatory, become systematic practices of repression and imprisonment in the process of their unfolding. These are the cases in which people, while striving for the fulfillment of their desires, accomplish something external to these desires, something antithetical to them. Hegel would call such situations 'the cunning of Reason', realizations of an inviolable historical rule governing the destinies of people, nations and states.

On the other hand, it is possible to explain such transformations through the influence of the unconscious. The cases when revolutions degenerate are those in which conscious desire for liberation is accompanied by unconscious desire for enslavement or submission. The more the desire for liberation is satisfied, the more is dissatisfaction with the delay in the execution of another, secret desire, and hence the urge to satisfy it grows.

This may also be the case when individuals or small communities attempt to reclaim the history of the arts for themselves.[18] What if the desire to use history as an instrument of liberation is accompanied by an unconscious desire to make it an implement of repression? It is reasonable to expect such an opportunity, if only to make sure that art historians with

---

18 For more detailed discussion of this topic see: Kolomiets G. "What Governs the History of Art?" // *Rêvenance* #1, p. 6

emancipatory intentions do not have such unconscious desires, and that the appropriation of history for personal needs is necessarily carried out with motivations of freedom, rather than oppression.

An analysis of the unconscious of a historian is a complex task. First of all, there is the problem of access to this unconsciousness. The mere fact that the result of the historian's activity is text raises many questions about the possibility of access to the unconsciousness through the text. How to separate elements of a text that appear as a result of conscious action from those that originate from a historian's unconscious? Can a text give the same kind of access to the unconsciousness as the subject's speech (psychoanalysis), behavior (behaviorism) or the scientific picture of physiological functions (neuropsychology)? Can the writing as such contain unconscious elements?

Questions of this kind indicate that the attainment of external access to a historian's unconscious is either a difficult or virtually impossible task. Therefore, for tactical reasons, it seems valid to use not the external 'psychoanalysis' of a historian, but his self-analysis: before beginning the appropriation of history, it is reasonable to make sure that it is not intertwined with interests of oppression. Therefore, it is important to find a procedure that would help us to identify the influence of our unconscious on our own historical discourse.

Hints for finding at least one of the possible elements of such a procedure are found in Michel Foucault's *Archaeology of Knowledge*. The philosopher begins to develop his archaeology by removing from the historical discourse a number of concepts - tradition, influence, development, evolution and 'spirit'.[19] Foucault characterizes these concepts as "ready-made syntheses, <...> groupings that we normally accept before any examination, <...> links whose validity is recognized from the outset".[20] Thus, Foucault discovers in historical methodology a

---

19 *The Archaeology of Knowledge*, trans. A.M. Sheridan Smith (New York: Routledge, 2002) – pp. 23-24.

20 Ibid., p. 24.

set of concepts that are used out of habit, without preliminary discussion, without justification of their pressing need for historical research – and therefore unconsciously.

Moreover, Foucault characterizes the concepts he eliminates as directed towards identification of various historical phenomena and their totalization within the framework of an abstract scheme. For example, the purpose of the concept of tradition is "... to give a special temporal status to a group of phenomena that are both successive and identical (or at least similar); it makes it possible to rethink the dispersion of history in the form of the same; it allows a reduction of the difference proper to every beginning, in order to pursue without discontinuity the endless search for the origin; tradition enables us to isolate the new against a background of permanence, and to transfer its merit to originality, to genius, to the decisions proper to individuals".[21]

This kind of hierarchization can be compared with the hierarchization of the subjects of power within a totalitarian state - the differences between them are eliminated in order to identify their identities as citizens subordinate to the government in the same degree, with all spheres of life equally open to observation, control and management. One can continue this analogy and say that a historian using 'ready-made' concepts unconsciously contributes to the establishment of power relations organized on the totalitarian principle within the historical discourse. Of course, the practice of tyrannical power differs from the practice of the historian's ordering of abstract, inanimate phenomena of the past. But on the other hand, one of the self-evident, in my opinion, signs of totalitarianism is deprivation of citizens' human rights, neglect of their qualities of independent autonomous individuals, which leads to turning them into abstract inanimate objects of governance.

Foucault's methodology with the concepts of historical discourse can also be used when we reclaim art history for ourselves – it could be important to establish which of the concepts used by a historian are accepted as necessary by default, habitually, unconsciously.

---

21 Ibid., p. 23.

Having discovered these concepts, the historian can consider their inherent modes of the hierarchization of historical phenomena, which, in turn, can be analyzed from the point of view of power relations, as well as tactical and strategic goals of their application.

If it turns out that the conscious intention of the historian to bring history out of the totalitarian academic structures is accompanied by an unconscious desire to establish his own undivided power over history, it is reasonable to refuse to use these concepts or, at any rate, to change their content in such a way that their way of ordering of historical phenomena will take non-repressive forms.

~^~^~^~^~^~^~^~^~^~^~^~^~^~^~^~^~^~^~^~^~^~^~^~^~^~^~^~^~^~

**Translator's note:** *In every era, there are precursors to the disasters to come; and they always come. Disasters which are as inevitable and as inexorable as the foregone conclusions of a classical Greek tragedy. In every age there are voices unheeded that sound the clarion-call to defend, to shelter, to flee. Our own turbulent epoch is no exception. If only we had ears to hear the neglected Cassandras whose cries we mute with our indifference…*

## Glas (1897)
### *by Ivan Gilkin*

O cloches lourdes, cloches lentes,
    Dolentes,
    Râlantes,

Cloches des sinistres journées,
    Damnées,
    Damnées,

Cloches de deuil, cloches d'alarmes
    En armes,
    En larmes,

O cloches de sang, cloches d'âcres
    Massacres,
    Massacres,

## Knell (1897)
### *by Ivan Gilkin*

O heavy bells, sluggish bells,
    Mournful,
    Maddening,

Bells of evil days,
    Condemned,
    Condemned,

Bells of grief, alarm bells
    Armed,
    In tears,

O bells of blood, bitter bells,
    Slaughter,
    Slaughter,

O cloches, cloches, cloches, cloches,
        Plus proches,
        Plus proches,

Sonnez, cloches, cloches funèbres,
        Ténèbres !
        Ténèbres !

Voici que dans l'air qui s'étonne,
        Il tonne,
        Il tonne !

Sous les neiges de flamme comme
        Sodome,
        Sodome,

Périssent les cités infâmes
        En flammes
        En flammes !

Cloches sur les maisons où monte
        La honte,
        La honte,

Cloches sur l'église où les râbles
        Des diables,
        Des diables,

Remplacent pour l'Eucharistie
        L'hostie,
        L'hostie,

Sonnez sur le meurtre et l'inceste
        La peste,
        La peste,

Et sur la Foi qui s'effémine,
        Famine,
        Famine,

O bells, bells, bells, bells,
        Nearer,
        Nearer,

Ring, bells, funereal bells,
        Shadows !
        Shadows !

Here in the air which astounds itself,
        Roaring,
        Roaring !

Beneath the snows of fire like
        Sodom,
        Sodom,

Destroying the infamous cities
        In flames
        In flames !

Bells upon the houses where rises
        Shame,
        Shame,

Bells on the church where the rabble
        Of devils,
        Of devils,

Replace the Eucharist
        The host,
        The host,

Toll upon murder and incest
        Plague,
        Plague,

And upon the Faith which emasculates itself,
        Famine,
        Famine,

| | |
|---|---|
| Et sur l'envie et la colère | And upon envy and hate |
| La guerre, | War, |
| La guerre | War |
| | |
| Mais nul n'écoute vos reproches, | But your reproaches are unheeded, |
| O cloches, | O bells, |
| O cloches, | O bells, |
| | |
| Et c'est en vain que pour personne, | And it is in vain that for anyone, |
| Je sonne, | I toll, |
| Je sonne ! | I toll ! |

*Translated by Raymond E. André III;* from Ivan Gilkin, *La Nuit.* (1897) Fischbacher: Paris.
~^~^~^~^~^~^~^~^~^~^~^~^~^~^~^~^~^~^~^~^~^~^~^~^~^~^~^~^~^~^~

*The Symbolist journal* **Mercure de France**, *begun by Alfred Valette using his bedroom as an editorial office, eventually grew into one of the largest and most influential literary reviews in France; it published work by Jarry, Valéry, Apollinaire, Fort, and countless others. The reviewer in this brief article, Hirsch, had connections to both the Symbolist and Realist movements. By 1912, these movements had given birth to newer avant-gardes, whose infusion with Modernism has often blinded historians (and writers) to the corollary continuities.* **The following short review of Cravan's legendary self-published Maintenant** *(Now), which he vended out of a wheelbarrow in the streets of Paris, gives a glimpse of the older generation of the avant-garde's reaction to the first stirrings of what would soon become the Dada movement – one in which they seem to see progression rather than rupture. The* **Mercure** *printed the final stanza of the following poem with the review.*

# Review of *Maintenant* No. 1 (1912)
## *by Charles-Henry Hirsch*

Now (No. 1, April), "literary review", of a yet-secret periodicity, is a paper of 8 pages for presenting: Whistle, a poem of its director, Mr. Arthur Cravan, "Unpublished Documents on Oscar Wilde," signed W. Cooper, and two announcements of restaurants, of which one is a "house recommended to those gentlemen the students".

The verses of Mr. Arthur Cravan are those of a fervent disciple of Walt Whitman. They clearly indicate a poet anxious about the modern, and gifted with lyricism:

# Whistle (1912)

*by Arthur Cravan*

☐

The Atlantic's rhythm rocks the oceanliners,
And up in the air where the gasses dance so with the pinwheels
Whilst whistles the heroic express which arrives at Havre,
Press on like bears, the athletic sailors.
New York! New York! That's where I'd like to live!
There I see science marry
Industry,
In an audacious modernity.
And in the palaces
Globes,
Dazzling the retinas,
With their ultra-violet rays;
The American telephone,
the tender nature
Of elevators…

☐

The English Company's inspiring vessel
Saw me take my place aboard terribly excited,
And entirely delighted with the beautiful turbine vessel's amenities,
Like the installation of electricity,
Casting light in torrents on the throbbing cabin.
The cabin burning with copper jambs,
Upon which, in seconds, played my drunken hands
To shiver roughly in the metal's chill,
And douse my appetite in this plunging thrill,
All the while the green influence of the new varnish
Clearly screeched out the date, when, discarding the bills,
In the deranged green of the grass, I rolled like an egg.
How my shirt befuddled me! And to feel your shudder
In the style of a horse, at one with nature!
How I'd wanted to graze! How I'd wanted to run!
And how I was naturally on deck, battered by the music intense;
And how the cold is powerful as physical sense,

When you're striving to breathe!
Finally, unable to whinney, unable to swim,
I did my hobnobbing among the passengers,
and the tumbling waterline they kept their eyes on ;
And until we saw together the tramways* of morning head for the horizon,
And swiftly bleach the houses' facades.
Beneath the rain, and beneath the sun, and beneath the starry circus,
We sailed without mishap for seven times twenty-four hours!
☐


Commerce favored my youthful initiative:
Eight million dollars made in preserves
And the famous brand of Gladstone's head
Gave me ten steamers* of four thousand tons each,
Which fly flags embroidered with my initials,
And impress upon the waves my commercial power.
I possess as well my first locomotive:
It whistles its steam, like hair which is shaken free,
And, bending its pride beneath the professional fingers/rights,
It foolishly files, rigid on its eight wheels.
It hauls a long haul in its adventurous marches,
In green Canada, to the virgin forests,
And across my bridges upon caravans of arches,
To the sunrise, the fields and the familiar wheat;
Where, thinking to make out a town among the starry nights,
It whistles infinitely across the valleys,
While dreaming of an oasis: the station with the sky of glass,
In the undergrowth of the rails that it criss-crosses by the thousands,
Where, eying its cloud, it rolls its tonnage.


*Translated by Olchar Lindsann*
*with advice from Kala Ladenheim*

* *English in the original.*

from *Mercure de France*, Vol. 47, No.357. May 1, 1912.       from the Revenant Archive.
        & *Maintenant*, No. 1, April, 1912.
~^~^~^~^~^~^~^~^~^~^~^~^~^~^~^~^~^~^~^~^~^~^~^~^~^~^~^~^~^~

# A Mystery Correspondent!

In the first issue of **Rêvenance** I encouraged, "contributions that are humble in size, but striking in their interest or intriguing in their implications." Here's the first, which falls under 'intriguing'. It was posted from Scottsdale, Arizona I have no correspondents) from Dolores Read. She did indeed live in the city at one point, but (I am a researcher after all) turns out to have died 14 years ago, in 2003. So this is truly a Revenant. (Now, it's *postmarked* from a city where I *do* know someone, but I shall keep mum.) It contained no note or explanation, only an undated (1894 or '95) 16-page catalog of a scientific bookseller in Paris, stamped as property of the U.S. Mint Laboratory in Washington, DC. and containing checkmarks indicating the purchase of eight books – most on hypnotism. The Mint Lab must have had some pretty interesting experiments going . . . Here are the first and last pages.

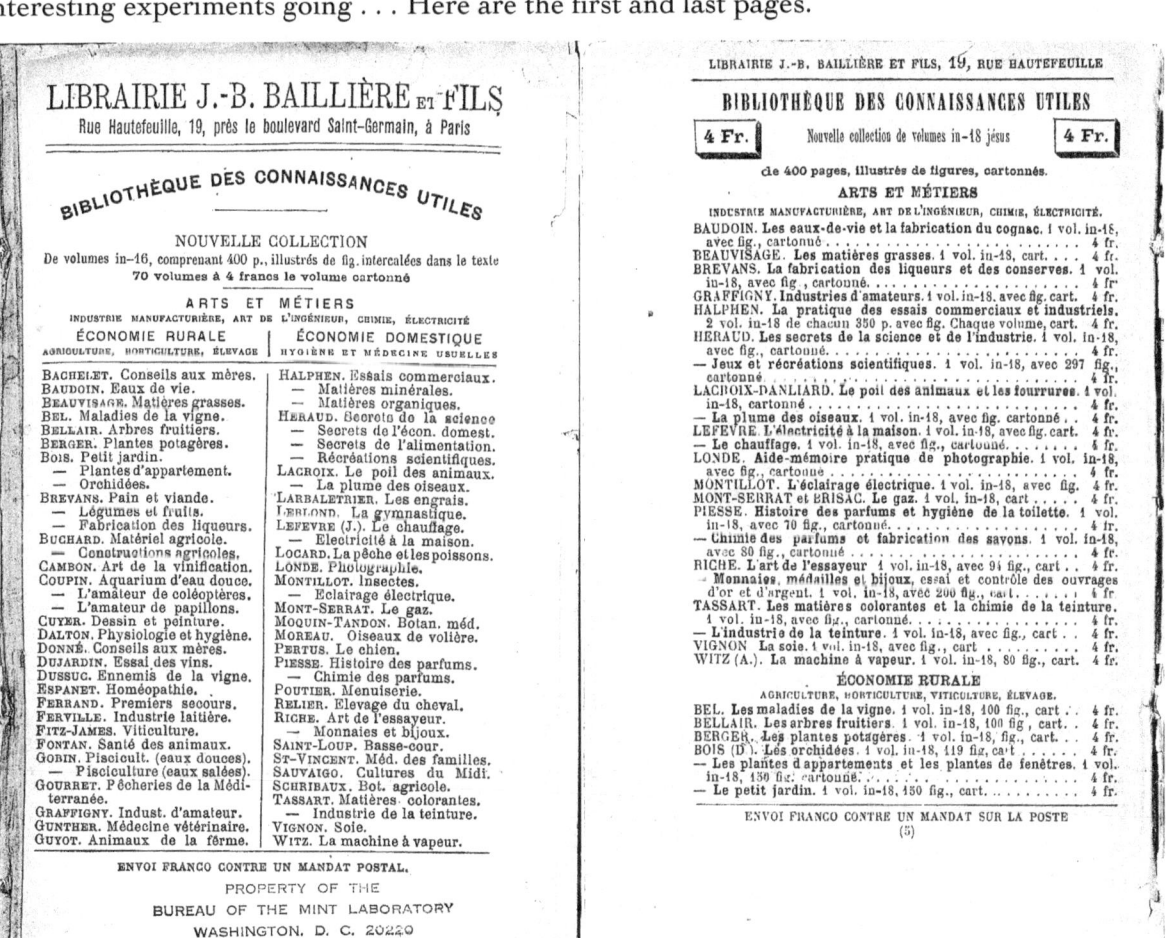

~^~^~^~^~^~^~^~^~^~^~^~^~^~^~^~^~^~^~^~^~^~^~^~^~^~^~^~^~^~^

# Lend your Eyes, Readers!

*This manuscript needs transcribed! Let us know what you think via email. The original of this intriguing handwritten note to his collaborator Adam is held by the Revenant Archive; initial opinions are split regarding the sections of our tentative translation between brackets. It has been suggested that the* **T** *might in fact be a hybrid of interposed letters, proto-asemic lettristic play; an intriguing idea. The tentative translation is on the left, the tentative french transcription on the right.*

*Francis Vielé-Griffin was born in Virginia, but lived for most of his life in France and never wrote in English. He was one of the most formally experimental poets of his generation. With Paul Adam, he co-edited the influential Symbolist-Socialist journal* **Entretiens***, which gave equal space to avant-garde culture and to Socialist news articles, essays and polemics, with heavy anarchist leanings. The note's precise date and context are not known.*

## [T?]rust (Undated, c. 1904)
### *by Francis Vielé-Griffin*

My favourite [book/cure]

Trust
because  unless i am deceived,
it is this first [book/cure] of inter-
psychology in which we could
see four populations yankee
Cuban, egyptian and french
spanned by one single idea,
modified by it, and
modifying it- in their turn, depending
on the nature of their elites and of
their masses in plain view.

Which has the most success
Trust

Mon [livre/cure] preferé

Le Trust
parceque si je ne m abuse,
c est ce premier [book/cure] d'inter-
psychologie où on puisse
voir quatre populations yankée
Cubaine, egyptienne et française
travserées par une même idee,
modifiée par elle, et la
modifiant- a leur tour, selon
les caractères de leur elites et de
leurs foules en pleine vie.

Lequel a eu le plus de succès
Le Trust

Mon livre préféré
        Le Trust

parceque si je ne m'abuse,
c'est le premier livre d'inter-
psychologie où l'on puisse
voir quatre populations yanti-
cubaine, égyptienne et française
traversées par une même idée,
modifiées par elle, et la
modifiant à leur tour, selon
les caractères de leur clités et de

leur foule en pleine vie.

Lequel a eu le plus de
    succès    Le Trust

The **Revenant Series** publishes translations, histories, and new editions of works related to the 19th Century avant-garde, including the Romanticist, Frenetic, Occultist, Utopian Socialist, Bohemian, Parnassian, Anarchist, Decadent, and Symbolist communities.

# New from mOnocle-Lash

*I, Engine: Collected and New Works, by Imogene Engine.* 102 pp. Engine's haunting, imagistic work has appeared (among other places) in nearly every collective publication of the Post-NeoAbsurdist movement since its founding 15 years ago. This collection, which includes both typeset and collaged poems, allows the intricate intertextuality of her oeuvre to emerge in all its fullness, revealing an intense and mysterious textual world teeming with depthless shadows and uncanny verbal collisions. *Introduction by Olchar Lindsann.*

*Permafrost, by Michael Dec.* 32 pp. Twenty-six new poems, running a startling gamut of themes, processes, and socio-verbal explorations. From Bennett's Preface: "You don't have to use scissors to cut up language, you can do it straight from your head, and Dec has achieved this in his excellent and long overdue new book, a book shining with complex, multi-layered, emotional, literary, and intellectual strengths." *Preface by John M. Bennet, Cover by Keith Higginbotham.*

## In Preparation for the mOnocle-Lash Revenants Series

*Soul-roulette: Transmutations of Nerval, by Gérard de Nerval and Retorico Unentesi.* Sound-based transductions of the Jeunes-France co-founder, carried out by Unentesi of the Kohoutenberg Institute for Study and Application; with an *extremely* extensive theoretical Appendix. *Fall 2017 Release.*

*Some Squibs, by Alphonse Allais.* Stories and poems by avant-satirist Allais (1854–1905): core member of the Hydropathes, Incoherents, and Chat Noir groups, painter of the first colour-field pictures, composer of the first soundless music score. *Winter 2017 release.*

*Philothée O'Neddy: Outlaw of Thought.* The first full-length collection in English of the Bouzingo co-founder, one of the most influential, yet forgotten, writers of the Romanticist avant-garde. Includes selections from his poetry, theory, fiction, criticism, & correspondence, memoirs by his friends and collaborators, plus a critical biography and bibliography, for the most comprehensive view of his total project ever published. *Tentative Summer 2018 release.*

Aug., A.Da. 101  /  A.H. 187  /  2017 C.E.

**mOnocle-Lash Anti-Press**
**REVENANT SERIES**
monoclelash.wordpress.com
monoclelash@gmail.com

# Rêvenance

## A Zine of Hauntings from Underground Histories

Issue No. 3          January 2018 (A.Da. 102, A.H. 188)

## Featuring

**The Dead**: Alphonse Allais / Théophile Gautier / Philothée O'Neddy / Gérard de Nerval / Thomas Hood / Célestin Nanteuil / Amable Tastu / Achille Devéria / Auguste Maquet / Alphonse Karr / Monte-Naken /Alboize de Pujol / Clarence G. Allen / Agnes Lee

**The Living**: Olchar E. Lindsann / Jim Leftwich / Sam Richards / Retorico Unentesi / Mr. Thursday

***Rêvenance*** is dedicated to the forgotten or untold histories of 19th Century avant-garde and dissenting countercultures. It promotes historiography practiced as game, as activism, as trans-generational collaboration, as communal memory, which running athwart the academic, refusing to describe history as finished, which does not stand apart to observe its object from a distance, in the posture of false 'objectivity' which Power always assumes. Instead: a *committed* historiography, which does not stand outside the stream of time or apart from its object: intellectual and precise, yet ludic and multi-form, one moment manifest as an essay, the next as a poem. A historiography created *within* the utopian fringe, and for the same community, responsive to our changing conditions, needs, and desires. A historiography that *we take personally*, merging imperceptibly into experiments in daily life, social praxis, and thought.

The journal is closely integrated with the Revenant Archive of roughly 500 books, prints, manuscripts, and personal items from the 19th Century avant-garde, and much of the material is drawn from the archive's material. The journal explores forgotten and newly-discovered histories of avant-garde, radical activist, utopian, and other underground countercultures. While the primary focus is on the 19th Century, earlier and later material is also welcome, and contributions directly connecting counter-cultural movements and strategies across time are particularly encouraged. The primary goal is to explore histories, communities, and themes that are not consistently represented elsewhere. ***Rêvenance*** seeks to develop a community of independent DIY researchers who see historical work as part of a communal praxis directed toward contemporary and future change; it is a laboratory in which countercultural history is transmuted, reflected and disseminated in the current lifestyle, writing, music, art, and thought of present-day communities of dissent or otherness.

**Edited by Olchar E. Lindsann**
*Rights retained by translators & living writers*
All other texts in the public domain
Lindsann's translations: Creative
Commons, Non-Commercial Share-Alike;
please inform us of republications

Aug., A.Da. 101
A.H. 187
2017 A.D.

**mOnocle-Lash Anti-Press**

## Revenants Series

monoclelash.wordpress.com
monoclelash@gmail.com

revenant-archive.blogspot.com
bouzingo.blogspot.com

Post: c/o Olchar Lindsann, Editor / 2027 Mountain View Terrace SW / Roanoke, VA 24015 / USA (**U**nfortunate, **S**ad **A**nathema)

# CONTENTS

*Many of the source texts are available online at* gallica.bnf.fr *and/or at* archive.org.

**Cover image by Olchar E. Lindsann**, collaged from: Célestin Nanteuil, *Portrait of Théophile Gautier* (1838) & *Gargantua* (c.1840-50), David d'Angers & Edmond Lechevallier-Chevignard, *Medallion Portrait of Achille Devéria* (Undated, c.1845-1857), *Photograph of Auguste Maquet* (c.1879), and anonymous masthead illustration to *Le Charivari*, Vol. 3, No. 50 (19 Feb., 1831). All constituent images are photocopied from original editions held in the Revenant Archive (not sliced up!).

**Send Submissions & Correspondence to monoclelash@gmail.com**

# Forward

In the course of editing each issue of *Rêvenance*, certain themes tend to emerge, but especially so with issue 3. The contributions of Hood, Allen, Allais and Karr explore the complex relationships between creative counterculture and what the Situationists later named the Spectacle. Karr and Tastu take us back to the vibrant Parisian underground community of the 1830s, to whom much of the remainder of the issue is dedicated. The centre of the issue is occupied by members of the Jeunes-France or Bouzingo group: a hypertextual poem by Gautier (plus a rant), then three reflections of the group's involvement with Libertine subculture by Maquet (with Pujol), Devéria (via contemporary avant-Libertine Mr. Thursday), and O'Neddy, then a charming note by Nanteuil (who also boasts three images throughout the issue), followed by a Nerval poem transducted by Unentesi. Leftwich and Richards advance poetic practices of Chronicling, recording the life of one creative community (Art Rat, where Lindsann & Thursday from this issue appear) and the communal assassination of another (Dartington, where the Rêvenance project began). A review and a forgotten poet close us out.

~^~^~^~^~^~^~^~^~^~^~^~^~^~^~^~^~^~^~^~^~^~^~^~^~^~^~^~^~^~^~^~

*The seeds of the contemporary "Art Market" were the Art Unions of the early 19th Century, which functioned on the corporate model: members paid shares, which were pooled and used to invest in works of contemporary art; these works (now functioning merely as abstract investments, not as intellectual functions or aesthetic objects) were then distributed back to investors by means of a raffle. The leftist poet and satirist Thomas Hood pondered:*

## On the Art Unions  (1843)
### *by Thomas Hood*

> That picture-raffles will conduce to nourish
> Design, or cause good coloring to flourish,
> Admits of logic-chopping and wise sawing,
> But surely Lotteries encourage Drawing!

from *The New Monthly Magazine and Humorist*. 1843. ed. Thomas Hood. Colburn: London.

~^~^~^~^~^~^~^~^~^~^~^~^~^~^~^~^~^~^~^~^~^~^~^~^~^~^~^~^~^~^~^~

*The development of art and literary consumerist markets, and the* professionalisation *that accompanied them, did not go uncontested. The first true Zine network – non-commercial pamphlets printed by (often adolescent) amateurs in tiny editions on personal reproduction devices at home to be traded, rather than sold, through a network that spanned both local and postal communities – was known as the* **Amateur Press** *movement. (The term came nearly a century later) It began forming during the 1860s in America, and in 1876 the* **National Amateur Press Association** *was founded; self-declared non-professionals traded their home-printed pamphlets through massive mailing lists, like the later mail art and zine networks. This decidedly amateur, yet goofy and revealing, poem was printed by the teenage Clarance Allen in one of the most influential of these early zines,* **The Crucible**, *that very year, and shows that even before the official Association – and nearly a century before the more confrontational zine culture of Riot Grrl and Punk – an extensive community of underground micropublishing was flourishing;* **The Crucible** *was one of at least 30 amateur periodicals being published in Washington D.C. at the time, as spoofed here.*

## A Living Phenomenon   (1876)
### *by Clarence G. Allen*

As I walked down the Avenue
  A day or two ago,
I met a boy whose puckered face
  Gave evidence of woe.
His grimy knuckles rubbed his eyes,
  The tears poured forth apace,
And plowed their furrowed path adown
  His dirty little face.
He lifted up his voice to weep –
  Ah, what a voice he had!
I wondered what the trouble was
  That made him feel so bad.
I thought perchance that stomach-ache
  His youthful form might rack, [sic]
Or that his father with a gad
  Had warmed his little back.
A kindly impulse stirred my heart,
  I took him by the hand,

And asked the reason of his grief
  In accents kind and bland.
"Say, whence these tears, my little son,
  And why this loud lament?
Hast thou been lashed about thy stern
  By some stern pa-ri-ent?
"Or has to strong a hankering
  For lollypop or cake
Convulsed thy little abdomen
  With throes of stomach-ache?"
He struggled for a moment hard,
  And then his sobs controlled;
And this is word for word the tale
  The little outcast told:–
"If you were in my place, old chap,
  You'd holler too, I guess,
"I'm the only boy in Washington
  What hain't no printing press!"

from *The Crucible: Devoted to the Reformation of Amateur Journalism*. Vol. I, No. 3 (March 15, 1876). Self-Published: Washington, D.C.　　From the collection of the Revenant Archive.

~^~^~^~^~^~^~^~^~^~^~^~^~^~^~^~^~^~^~^~^~^~^~^~^~^~^~^~^~^~^~

*One of the drawbacks of the celebrity culture that came to surround iconic artists and writers (alive or dead) within the commercial market during the 19<sup>th</sup> Century was that even complicated projects of dissent could end up popularized,* idolised, *reduced to stereotypes ("tics, tics, tics," as Ducasse says), and turned into pretexts for inanity. Alphonse Allais, who lived within the complicated grey area between mass culture and the avant-garde, demonstrates.*

# Drawbacks of Excessed Baudelairism[1]  (1893)
## by Alphonse Allais

Baudelaire's a must, got it, but you mustn't have too much. The anecdote which follows shall indicate, for the intelligent portion of my clientele, what one ought to take from Baudelairism and what it would be convenient to take a pass on.

A strapping young man, blond with an azure soul, learned his trade in an excellent pharmacy in Paris. His time was passed between official preoccupations and the reading, incessant, of *Flowers of Evil.*

Not one word whispered nearby; not one image evoked, not one iota whatsoever, see! would have failed to provoketh in his head, and in the rest of him, a verse or two by General Aupick's divine stepson.[2]

Now, one day, a lady came into the pharmacy and said to him:

— We have just, my husband and I, bottled some wine, but the content of the barrel is frightfully hazy, and I've come to ask you to give me a filter.

The young pill-slinger[3] handed over the filter.

Whether this filter was, in fact, composed of an unsturdy material, or the lady had, too brusquely, poured the liquid, the filter burst.

---

1   A neologism, outrancé, hence not "excessive", excessif.
2   Baudelaire's stepfather General Aupick was his constant nemesis.
3   *Potard.* According to Rigaud's *Dictionnaire d'argot moderne,* printed a few years earlier by Allais' own publisher Olendorff, *Potard* is slang for a Pharmacist or pharmacy student. The Decadent Huysmans is cited for the example.

And the lady returned to the pharmacy, saying to the young man:

– You don't have a sturdier filter?

So then, suddenly triggered by these words, the young Baudelairian declaimed:

> Ah, the best philters prescribed
> Are worth less than your idleness,
> And you have learned the caress
> Which can the dead revive![4]

Legitimately bent out of shape by this interpolative stanza which she had in no way merited, and which, let me tell you, she was far from prepared for, the lady went to recount the thing to her husband, who immediately set off to go administer to the etherial pill-slinger a thrashing black and blue.[5]

Was I not justified in stating from the start:

Baudelaire's a must, got it, but you mustn't have too much?

*Translated by Olchar E. Lindsann*

from Alphonse Allais, *Le Parapluie de l'Escuade*. 1893. Ollendorff: Paris.

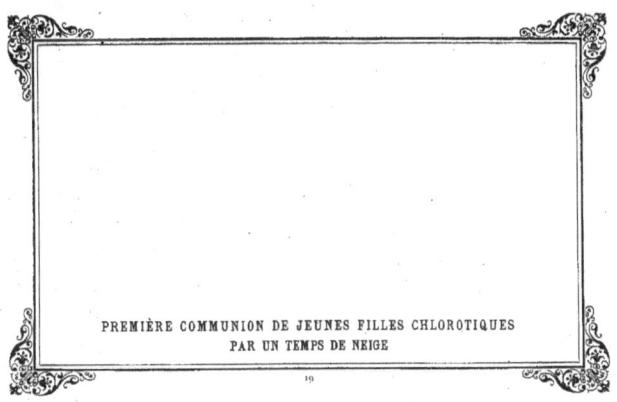

PREMIÈRE COMMUNION DE JEUNES FILLES CHLOROTIQUES
PAR UN TEMPS DE NEIGE

*Allais also created some of the most innovative visual art of his time, including one of the first series of abstract colour-field pictures such as that reproduced here:* **First Communion of Young Anaemic Girls in a Time of Snow** *(1883). Within the frame reproduced here was a blank sheet of paper.*

---

4    from Baudelaire's 'Chanson d'après-midi' (Afternoon Song)
5    *râclée noire.* The English expression, despite its added colour, seems to me closest to Allais' intention.

*Between 1830 and 1840, the figureheads of French Romanticism were turned swiftly from obscure intellectual iconoclasts into the first generation of rebels-turned-pop icons: proto rock stars, with fandoms and commercial spin-offs like the weird commodities described here in Karr's satirical avant-garde journal* **Les Guêpes***, which may or may not describe an actual product.*

# from **Les Guêpes** (1840)
## *by Alphonse Karr*

This year they've come up with some very ridiculous candies; – it's all the celebrated people in sugar stuffed with liquor. – I sent to someone yesterday for a Mrs. Sand in punch, – Mr. Hugo in maraschino, – Mr. Lamartine in rum, – Mrs. Rachel in kirschenwasser, – Mr. Chateaubriand in anisette, – Mr. Thiers in juniper berry, etc. etc.

Like bobbles, you hand countless of them over to children: – a Dupin in wood which wiggles the legs and arms in the middle of a string.

*-translated by Olchar E. Lindsann*

***A Set of Sweet Faces:*** *Notes/Portraits from Left to Right* – George Sand: Cross-dressing female Romanticist novelist / Victor Hugo: Figurehead of the Romanticist movement / Alphonse de Lamartine: Liberal Romanticist poet / Rachel: Leading Romanticist actress / René de Chateaubriand: Romanticist novelist & politician / Adolphe Thiers: Centrist politician. "Dupin" could be any number of public figures (it's even Sand's maiden name). Now, who wouldn't want to eat this crew?

from *Les Guêpes*, No. 3, Jan, 1840. Edited & written by Alphonse Karr. Self-Published, Paris. From the copy in the Revenant Archive.

~^~^~^~^~^~^~^~^~^~^~^~^~^~^~^~^~^~^~^~^~^~^~^~^~^~^~^~^~^~

*Amable Tastu was an early participant in Nodier's Romanticist salons at **the Arsenal,** and one of the most influential female poets of French Romanticism. Much of her work promoted the struggle for Greek independence and other Liberal causes of the time. After the 1830 Revolution, in which her husband's printing house was nearly bankrupted, her enthusiasm for democracy was temporarily dampened, but by 1848 she had co-founded, with a group of other Romanticist feminists, the **Society for the Mutual Education of Women**, which gave free literacy courses to working-class women throughout Paris and promoted gender-equal, democratic socialism.*

**The Profundities of Love,** *by Célestin Nanteuil (Undated, c.1835-70).*

# Groan (1838)
### *by Amable Tastu*

O world! o life! o time! phantoms, shades obscure,
Which fatigue my faltering steps until the end,
When shall those days return when your hands cradled more,
Your gaze so caressing, your covenant so sure?
　　Never, oh! never again!

Daylight is snuffed out in the tears wherein I drown;
The charms of the night pass unapprehended
Night, day, springtime, winter, can I savour nothing around?
My heart still beats with pain, but joyful pounds
　　Never, oh! Never again!

*Translated by Olchar E. Lindsann*

from Amable Tastu, *Poésies nouvelle.* 1838. Didier: Paris.

~^~^~^~^~^~^~^~^~^~^~^~^~^~^~^~^~^~^~^~^~^~^~^~^~^~^~^~^~^~^~

# A Rant & Object Lesson in Translation, Respect, & Romanticist Poetics
*A Poem by Théophile Gautier, a Rant by Olchar Lindsann, & Translations by him & Agnes Lee*

"From Apuleius filched"
*– Agnes Lee*

The following incredibly strange and complex little text by Théophile Gautier offers a fascinating insight into the remarkably refined poetics of quotation created and developed by the Romanticist avant-garde: this poem is an exhortation to research, it is a poetic re-working of Gautier's social and intellectual milieu. (Compare to Jim Leftwich's text later in this issue.)

Though (as he says) Gautier has never read Wordsworth, he's read enough of the second-generation English Romantics to realise that there is a tradition (Byron, Shelley, Hazlitt, et.al.) of *attacking* Wordsworth, and out of solidarity he attacks him as well. Rather brilliantly, he uses the single line he HAS read to spin a bibliographic web of references and resonances, allowing him to use the poem to ridicule one of the *Jeunes-France* group's own enemies, Jules Janin, who had likewise been attacked by Gautier's friends including his fellow co-founder, Petrus Borel and Alphonse Karr, from elsewhere in this issue.

There is one earlier translation of this poem by Agnes Lee, which is execrable; I make no grandiose claims for my own translation (I'm still learning the language), and am reticent to hurl stones at this glass house; yet I feel a duty on the part of Théo himself to protest. The publication in *Rêvenance* of experimental translations, transductions, etc. such as Unentesi's elsewhere in this very issue is testimony to the countless modes of translation available, and to their mutual value, but all demand, *in some form*, a respect for the writer, their text, and their contexts. This case demonstrates that importance.

In Lee's translation, none of these aspects of the text is respected: some lines are cut out entirely, others change position, and Apuleius is introduced into the poem for no reason at all besides having written a novel with the word 'ass' in it – albeit nearly two millennia years earlier. This is a perfect example of what happens when a translator or historian is uninterested in context, and pretends that 'The Poem' can be understood without reference to anything but itself. The problem is that Gautier designed this poem very carefully to be a pathway leading the reader to learn about the specific context he was working within; since (like most people who have dealt with Gautier in English) Lee clearly had no interest in the community he was writing for or the context he cared so much about, she declined to follow his trail of explicit clues and therefore failed even to recognise what the poem is actually *about*. Her translation and the original have been included for comparison.

To be fair, the poem is very complex. Gautier tells us that the line he quotes was found as an epigraph of a book, and he tells us the title. That's fairly simple, though Lee did not make it even that far (as we shall see). The line is the book's epigraph, just as Gautier tells us. As I found with a bit more research, the book is written under a pseudonym (as Gautier informs us), the name of a character of Janin's influential frenetic novel *The Dead Ass and the Guillotined Woman*, just as Gautier says. Anybody dealing with Gautier ought to recognize that title in the poem, given Janin's long-running battle with Gautier and his comrades.

Instead, Lee bypassed all of this—decided that since Apuleius had written a story called *The Golden Ass* (which admittedly was a favourite of the Romantics), and Gautier mentions the book called *The Dead Ass*, therefore the other novel mentioned, *Louisa*, MUST be by Apuleius, despite the fact that we know Apuleius never wrote such a novel. So, why not eliminate two whole lines from the poem, and then collapse the remains of the four stanzas into two?

Anyhow. Even beyond this careful intertextual architecture, the poem's mix of a casual, chatty tone, unwieldy technical bibliographic vocabulary, and more traditional poetic language make this a very virtuoso poem, drenched in bottomless irony, and is a hell of a challenge to render into verse in English translation; I've made use of a few tricks common in his verse. While I do not doubt that many flaws mar my own rendering, I hope that, at the very least, I haven't kicked his poem in the stomach like earlier translators – though I've perhaps kicked Agnes Lee as Théo kicked Janin and Wordsworth . . .

# A Line of Wordsworth's  (1832)
## by *Théophile Gautier*

### *Original French*

#### Un Vers de Wordsworth

*Spires whose silent finger points to heaven.*

Je n'ai jamais rien lu de Wordsworth, le poète
Dont parle lord Byron d'un ton si plein de fiel,
Qu'un seul vers ; le voici, car je l'ai dans la tête :
— *Clochers silencieux montrant du doigt le ciel.* —

Il servait d'épigraphe, et c'était bien étrange,
Au chapitre premier d'un roman : — *Louisa,* —
Les douleurs d'une fille, œuvre toute de fange
Qu'un pseudonyme auteur dans *L'Ane mort* puisa.

Ce vers frais et pieux, perdu dans ce volume
De lubriques amours, me fit du bien à voir :
C'était comme une fleur des champs, comme une plume
De colombe, tombée au cœur d'un bourbier noir.

Aussi depuis ce temps, lorsque la rime boite,
Que Prospéro n'est pas obéi d'Ariel,
Aux marges du papier je jette, à gauche, à droite,
Des dessins de clochers montrant du doigt le ciel.

***Translation #1*** by Olchar Lindsann

## *A Line of Wordsworth's*

*Spires whose silent finger points to heaven.*[6]


I've never ever read the poet Wordsworth, he
Against whom Lord Byron has let such venom fly,
'cept one line; here it is, for it comes back to me:
– *The silent steeples pointing to the sky.* –

It served as epigraph, and twas quite bizarre,
For the first chapter of the romance: – *Louisa,* – [7]
A daughter's afflictions, work thick with tar
Whose pseudonym an author from *The Dead Ass*[8] has seized.

This verse pious and fresh, abandoned in this book
Of embraces debauched, did me much good to find:
It was like a wild flower, like plumes shook
From a dove, upon a bog's black breast reclined.

And ever since that hour, when lame rhymes aren't deft,
And Ariel does not obey Prospero's cry,
Across the paper's margins I toss, to right, to left,
Several sketches of steeples pointing to the sky.

---

6   from *The Excursion*, Book VI, line 19.
7   *Louisa, ou les douleurs d'un fille de joie* (Louisa: or, a Prostitute's Pain), by Abbé Tiberge [Regnier-Destourbet].
8   *L'Ane Mort et la Femme guillotinée* (The Dead Donkey and the Guillotined Woman), by Jules Janin, 1829.

***Translation #2*** by Agnes Lee

## On a Thought of Wordsworth's

I've read no line of Wordsworth whom the Steven
   Of Byron hath assailed with bitterest gall,
    Save this I came upon, a fragment small
In a romance pseudonymously given,
From Apuleius filched, " Louisa," — leaven
   Of thought impure and pictures passional.
    How well the flash of beauty I recall,
The *"Spires whose silent finger points to heaven!"*

A white dove's feather down the darkness strayed,
   A lovely flower abloom in some foul nook.
    And now when riming halts and fancy tires,
And Prospero is of Ariel unobeyed,
   I over all the margin of my book
    Trace group on group of heavenward-pointing spires.

*Théophile Gautier, drawn by his fellow Jeunes-France co-founder, Célestin Nanteuil, in 1838.*

***Original from:*** Théophile Gautier, *Poésies Complète*, Vol. I. 1884. Charpentier: Paris. p. 111. This follows Gautier's preferred version in the Complete Works; the formatting is simpler in the first printing in *Albertus, ou L'âme et le péché: légende théologique*, 1833, by Paulin: Paris. p. 269.

***Translation #1*** by Olchar E. Lindsann.   ***Translation #2 from:*** Théophile Gautier, *Collected Works*, Édition Parisienne, Vol. 24: Enamels & Cameos, and Other Poems, trans. F.C. Sumichrast & Agnes Lee. 1903. Dumont: New York. p. 189.

~^~^~^~^~^~^~^~^~^~^~^~^~^~^~^~^~^~

*At sixteen years old, Auguste Maquet (aka Augustus Mac-Keat) was a co-founder of the seminal avant-garde* **Jeunes-France** *collective along with Gautier, Devéria, O'Neddy, Nerval, Clopet, and others; at eighteen he was teaching history at his former school, the prestigious Lycée Charlemagne. In addition to publishing novels under his own name, in 1838 he became a ghost-writer for Alexandre Dumas, and co-wrote* **The Three Musketeers** *and* **The Man in the Iron Mask***. His work on the latter drew directly on his ongoing historical research. Simultaneously he published a series of historical studies on the history of the French prison system, examined from a leftist perspective. His book on the Dungeon of Vincennes appeared the same year as his and Dumas'* **the Count of Monte Cristo***, also set largely in prison. His collaborator, Alboize Pujol, was a historian and playwright, and was the director of the Montmartre Theatre; he may have been the son of the Classicist painter Abel Pujol.*

# Libertines & Revolutionaries in the French Prisons (1844)
## *by Auguste Maquet & Alboize du Pujol*

**From *History of the Dungeon of Vincennes*:**

Not all prisons are alike. Perhaps there shall come a day when they are all alike; but when we climb back into the past to study this question in the monuments that still remain, we see the traces of force more clearly than those of the law, and we find far more ideas of revenge than ideas of restraint. Moreover the design and construction of prisons are in proportion to the power or pride of their founders. We perceived in the Bastille everything that Aubriot meditated against his enemies. The purpose of this monument was unequivocal. The Bastille could only serve, in the architect's mind, to repulse the enemies from without and to torture them efficiently within whenever the aggressors should become prisoners.

But Vincennes can be considered from other perspectives. It is a consoling notion to the historian, that this imposing mass should not have been tossed up solely for the suffering of men; certainly, the results have been the same for Vincennes as for the Bastille, and while spinning in the vicious circle of despotism, the kings of France ended up erecting prisons here where they had wanted to erect palaces; but Vincennes' beginnings were unconnected to this sombre hue which darkened the stones, when still new, of the Saint-Antoine fortress. Perhaps even when we carefully strip off these many layers of accumulated chronicles, which form public opinion over time, we see that the palace of Vincennes must owe to this innocent origin having been less despised than the Bastille. The woods and flowers made it through the iron and stone.

That beautiful forest of Vincennes is one of the most ancient to gratify the pride of the Isle-de-France, formerly blanketed in woods. The Romans erected there a little temple as well as a school consecrated to the god Silvanus; the remains of this monument lasted for a long time as a priory in the Vincennes forest . . .

[ . . . ]

The publication of this work [*On Executive Orders and State Prisons*][9], which preceded that of Linguet on the Bastille, was more powerful, as it needed to be. More energetic, more eloquent, more logical and above all more sweeping than the latter, that of Mirabeau addresses the entire question of individual liberty, stemming from the usurpation carried out by the kings and the people in power of their subject's persons, undermining the basic rights allocated to them, he commits  himself to the resistance and names this sacred revolt whose name is changed into revolution; Linguet limits himself to dealing with the Bastille's administration . . . One often sees, as we have shown, upright in the dungeon's lantern, the eyes fixed upon Paris, that immense town where he seeks the cradle of liberty, tossing them to the wind, in the hope that it would carry them to the Parisians, these words drawn from his *Essay on Despotism*:

> We, descendants of those proud Gauls, whose valour was nourished at the breast of liberty and ceaselessly animated by her, who wrested from the roman historians the admission of the dread that they inspired in Rome, so accustomed to seeing its consuls and legions humiliated by this bellicose people, that the proud senate, judge and protector of kings, 'thought only of its security and forgot its glory, whenever it had to combat these redoubtable enemies;' we, beneath the blows from which are cut down the wild despo-

---

9   *Des Lettres de Cachet et des prisons d'état.* Published in 1782 after Mirabeau's release. Probably a major influence on Maquet's and his collaborator Pujol's historiography in this project.

tism which makes the universe grovel, we allow to flee from our breast this liberty which gave our fathers their glorious renown and the lengthy period of a vast and flourishing empire! . . . Virtuous men, struggle on behalf of this sacred liberty!

But the echoes were faint of these words which were lost in space; a day arrived nonetheless when, exchanging this tribunal for that of the National Assembly, his powerful voice resounded throughout Europe, encouraged the people and made the kings blanche. The great orator then loved to recall the essays which he had composed on the summit of the dungeon, and blessed the orator's apprenticeship, begun in chains.

The *Executive Orders*[10] were not the only work that Mirabeau composed during his detention. Since Mr. Lenoir had authorised his correspondence with Sophie, his passion for her seemed to have redoubled its violence means of privation and satisfaction. Tormented by the sensory tumult that his strong physical constitution exacerbated, he devoted himself to a work which became the reflection of everything he experienced as it passed. The commentaries of don Clamet on the Bible inspired him with the idea to entitle it: *The Erotica-Biblion. It assembles within a single framework all the bizarre tastes of men, all the means they have employed to diversify their pleasures, outwitting nature and creating new passions.* This unique and original work required great research which renders it quite authoritative; but the obscene style which prevailed there revealed the author's motives too much. They can only be excused by his particular situation, and we had to mention it in order to reveal Mirabeau's constitution; he merited furthermore, on behalf of one of his friends, the following letter: "Necessity," said he, "ought not force a man to lack respect for himself, and it is not poison that he needs to sell to earn his bread."

[ . . . ]

Mirabeau had as a companion in captivity the famous count de Sade, about whom he had already been questioned in the Bastille. We know that the cynical writings and actions, the brazen libertinage, the famous meal of cantharides in Marseille,[11] finally going as far as incest,

---

10 *Lettres de cachet*
11 Sade had been found guilty (in absentia) of sodomy, outrage to public morals, and attempt-

were the motives for his captivity. This prisoner, who since the 30th of October was incarcerated successively in the house of Chauffour, in that of Saumer, in the Conciergerie, in Pierre-en-Clise, was locked up in Vincennes on February 13th 1777; he remained there until February 29th 1784, at which point he was transferred to the Bastille, where we tell his story.

### from *History of the Bastille:*

The Bastille's last order of extradition that we find on the registers is that of the marquis de Sade. This powerful lord, placed in Vincennes in the first place *for inhuman experiments that they accused him of having done in Provence upon living individuals,* as put down in the column for causes of detention, was transferred to the Bastille, February 29th 1784, with the count de Solanges, de Wythe and others, when they disgorged this prison. The marquis de Sade, who, if he was guilty of the crime that they accused him of, merited a severe punishment, was on the contrary treated with less severity than the others. They permitted him to wallpaper his cell, which was the third room in the Liberty tower; they permitted him moreover, upon his payment, to have a good time. He also enjoyed the favor of taking strolls on the towers. Toward the middle of the month of June 1789 the troubles which had taken place in the faubourg Saint-Antoine, around the Bastille, concerned [the prison's governor] Mr. de Launay, who subsequently took the precaution of having the canon loaded and forbidding the marquis de Sade's strolls on the towers. He, scarcely satisfied with the reasons given to him for prompting this interdiction, lost his head at the governor, and warned the aforementioned Lassinotte, his turnkey, that if in one hour he did not have a favourable response to the request to the governor with which he charged him, he would stir up a riot that would rouse all Paris. The governor persisted in his refusal, and the marquis de Sade persisting in his disquisition, took a tin pipe which ended in a funnel and which had been made in order for him

---

ed poisoning – the latter stemming from his feeding prostitutes a popular aphrodisiac, cantharides (or Spanish Fly).

to pass his water more efficiently into the ditch, and this serving for him as a kind of mega-phone, appealed to the common people for aid, vomiting out his grievances against Mr. de Launay, whom he accused of wanting to assassinate him. His shouting was in fact heard in the street and in the faubourg Saint-Antoine. They gathered, they rioted, and perhaps were about to attempt what actually happened a month later, when the shouting ceased, and night having fallen everyone retired, but went away with the thought that there currently existed victims of the Bastille. At the first shouts, Mr. de Launay had rushed into the marquis de Sade's prison and made him go down into the [officially sanctioned] path by promising him for tomorrow the walk that he had been refused today. But overnight he sent an express to Versailles, and at daybreak the marquis was transferred to Charenton.

Any other prisoner would have been submitted to solitary confinement and other most cruel positions; but the marquis de Sade was a powerful lord who had only been accused of a crime more vile than theft, more atrocious than assassination; they dared not clamp down on him, they contented themselves with transferring him to another prison where his shouts could pose no danger.

Thus the final act of the Bastille presented this monstrosity of despotism, that too cruel for a wrongly-accused man, it became the refuge for a guilty one, whom it ended up shielding from justice. In so doing so it was returned to its initial origin; it was with this two-fold reali-sation of the arbitrary that they tore down its foundations.

It is under this two-fold aspect that we have written its history here.

*Translated by Olchar E. Lindsann*

from Auguste Maquet & Alboize du Pujol, *Le Donjon de Vincennes, Faisant suite `L'Histoire de la Bastille depuis sa fondation jusqu-a nos jours.* (1869) Bunel: Paris. Edition from the Revenant Archive – pp.1-2, 224-6, & 236-7; and from Maquet, Pujol, & Auguste Arnould, *Histoire de la Bastille, depuis sa fondation 1374 jusqu'a sa destruction 1789.* 1844. Administration de Librairie: Paris – pp. 196-7.

~^~^~^~^~^~^~^~^~^~^~^~^~^~^~^~^~^~^~^~^~^~^~^~^~^~^~^~^~^~^~^~^~^~^~^~

# *from* **Diabolical Fucko Mania (c.1835)**

*by Achille Devéria    Commentary by Mr. Thursday*

*Diabolico Foutro Manie; Diabolical Fucko Mania* (DFM), is a series of twelve lithographic prints by Achille Devéria, published likely in a folio, c. 1835. "Develries" and "diableries" in verse, prose, print or novelty form were in a heightened state of demand during the Romanticist period and the advent of lithography advanced their promulgation in image form. DFM, a meditation on the morality of the Louis-Philippe regime, sees elite/bourgeois men and women as participants and prey in a cascade of fiendishly prurient, excremental, slap-stick offenses against decent living,

proper love, and high society. Platoons of imps, perverted faeries, mutants and devils — one wonders if this horde represents King Louis-Philippe's effect or romanticist/decadent intervention — are active in every nook of life.

In keeping with the theme of Romanticist erotico-diabolic incu/succubi, here is offered the sixth image in the DFM series. A bourgeois woman collaborates with a devilish man, perhaps M. Satan himself, coiffed in a Flame of Glory. Under the desk mutual service unfolds, unbeknownst, perhaps, to the bespectacled (?) caretaker (?) reading in the background.

It is impossible not to see this darkling humor and enjambed composition surviving in Rops, Beardsley, von Bayros, Van Maele, Finland, InCase and Chriss.

~^~^~^~^~^~^~^~^~^~^~^~^~^~^~^~^~^~^~^~^~^~^~^~^~^~^~^~^~^~^~^~

The poet Philothée O'Neddy (aka Théophile Dondey) was a co-founder of the **Jeunes-France** or **Bouzingo** group along with Devéria, and one of the most influential writers of the very early avant-garde. This poem from his seminal (and only) collection of poetry, **Fire and Flame**, embodies the libidinal, neuralgic, gothic energy of Frenetic Romanticism, from which Baudelaire, Lautréamont, the Decadents and Surrealists drew heavy inspiration, and includes poems such as "Spleen", "Dandyism", and "Neuralgia", which became key terms and themes in 19th Century counterculture. The poem's epigraphs cite his fellow Bouzingos Alphonse Brot and Théophile Gautier; refer to the translation and commentary on Gautier's own use of epigraphs on pp 10-13. The first full-length English-language anthology of O'Neddy's work is currently under preparation.

# Succubus  (1833)

## by Philothée O'Neddy

@@@@@@@

"She was worth a whole seraglio!"
Théophile Gautier

"What! you wish to delay the moment of happiness!"
Alphonse Brot.

~~~~~~~


I dreamed only, last night, storms splendidly endowed,
Upon the pitching floor of a salon of clouds,
By terror and love relentlessly contorted,
With a Bohemian girl slim and lustful there
In a waltz danced in the air,
Drunk on madness, I was transported.

As if my arms enclosed her unreal waist!
And a breast by supple velvet was embraced
Oh! as if I inhaled her provoking scents!
And how I was inflamed, when, abrupt and savage,
The wind unfurled around my visage
Her brown locks hurled in torrents!

Surely there inhered pleasure and poetry
In the infernal spasm, the chill frenzy,
Luxurious thrill, corroding it to blight,
Which gnawed, tormented our shuddering souls,
Twisting so much on the clouds' pliant folds
    That underfoot we felt their flight!

Oh! Pity!—I am dying—Pity! my sylph neuralgic!
Said I in a voice expiring, electric.

Observe—my whole frame throbbing incandescent—
Come, come, we'll scale a star, secrete ourselves inside;
—And there, shall your beauty unveiled cease to hide
    From my fervent adolescence!

Mad laughter seizes her... such discordant laughs,
Fit to spread over the satanic repast
—I was convulsed, my teeth were spitting stridence—
Suddenly, no more sprite of lustful ablution!
    Naught in my arms but a skeleton
    Flaunting all her repugnance!

Oh! Thus your love delights your dancer's interest!
Whispered her rasping voice. And her osseous chest
Panted with her desire, palpitated with lust.
And always, always then, from cloud to cloud,
    With her by the torrent endowed
    I was upthrust in my disgust!

In order to be cleansed of this lasciviousness,
I fought fruitlessly in the anaemic mist:
With her angular arms the entanglement fierce
Became encrusted in my flesh where fever dripped,
And the sharp kisses of her mouth without lips
　　My cheek and my forehead pierced.

As if in farewell, in my dark wretchedness,
Suddenly I cried out the name of my mistress…
What treasure in that name! what divine amulet!
The ghost released me from orb to orb to go.
—And, glad to awaken, I caressed my theorbo,
　　Necromancer's instrument.

*Translated by Olchar E. Lindsann*

from Philothée O'Neddy, *Feu et flamme*. 1833. La Librairie orientale de Dondey-Dupré.

~^~^~^~^~^~^~^~^~^~^~^~^~^~^~^~^~^~^~^~^~^~^~^~^~^~^~^~^~^~^~^~

# An Avant-Romanticist Dinner Invitation  (1845)
## *by Célestin Nanteuil*

*Célestin Nanteuil and Léon Clopet were co-founders of the* **Jeunes-France** *group around 1829 (along with Gautier, Maquet, O'Neddy, and Nerval, all in this issue, among others). Clopet was a successful architect who had funded much of the group's activity, Nanteuil was the leading illustrator of the Romanticist movement. He was also the figurehead of the Medievalist tendency within the nascent avant-garde, not only in his experimental re-invention and radicalization of medieval visual culture, but also in his daily life by means of adopting  medieval furniture (cheap at the time), costumes, and modes of speech. This dinner invitation shows how role-playing and word-play were still central to their friendship and daily lives more than a decade after the group's public activity ceased. It also shows this subculture being passed on to the next generation, for the rest of the party consists of younger Romanticist illustrators for whom Nanteuil was both a mentor and frequent collaborator. They were part of an influential movement of progressive satire that would have important effects on both cartooning and politics throughout the 19th Century.*

## from Célestin Nanteuil to Léon Clopet; montalais, June 2, 1845.

~~~~~~~~~~~~~~~~~~~~

### Order of Service

Sir Léon, commander in chief of the Clog and second in command of the Chick,[12] shall report next Saturday for Bougival at half past four at the railroad upon the right-hand side. Having arrived in Bougival, he shall be recognised by the captain of the Frog[13], who shall request that he consume the soup which shall appear upon the table at precisely six at the abode of Sousent.[14] He shall encounter those known as Arcy, Français, Leleux, and Baron, together with the aforementioned captain.[15] He shall retire to bed at a very goodly hour after having been conveyed in the same fashion and arrive as early as possible on Sunday morning in view of the cape of Bellevue.

[Signed:]

The Captain of the Frog, Célestin Nanteuil

*Translated by Olchar E. Lindsann*

From *Lettres Autographes composant la collection de M. Alfred Bovet.* ed. Alfred Bovet & Étienne Charavay. 1885. Librairie Charavay Frères: Paris. p. 606.

---

12 *sabot*, wooden shoe still worn by French peasants at the time, and Cocotte, "chicken" but used for a variety of affectionate slang ranging from a cute child to that corresponding to the chauvinist "chick" in American or "hen" in the UK.

13 A printmaking pun: *grenouille* is also a term for the part of a printing press which receives and distributes the pressure.

14 *chez Sousent*. This individual has yet to be identified.

15 François-Louis Français, a landscape painter associated with the Barbizon school; Adolphe Pierre Leleux, another painter who counted several other ex-bouzingo among his friends, including Nerval and Gautier; and the romanticist illustrator Henri Baron, whose premier as a painter had been a collaborative canvas with Français, and was a very frequent collaborator with Nanteuil on various illustration projects; Arcy (or d'Arcy) remains unidentified.

***Gargantua***, *by Célestin Nanteuil (Undated, c.1840–50). In this avant-Romanticist "portrait" of Rabelais' medieval satirical character, Gargantua's head and body has been replaced with a scene of the industrializing city of Paris as a collapsing colonial vortex drawing in people and goods from across the world. The skewed perspective, refusal of illusionistic depth and scale, and the compositional emphasis on the frame reflect Nanteuil's radicalisation of medieval aesthetics.*

# Vers Dorés / Golden Tooth

*by Gérard de Nerval, mutagenic (mis)translation by Retorico Unentesi*

*Unentesi-the-translator can be found (along with many other marginal characters) at the intersection of an improvisational historiography (always in part a partially-regretted nostalgia for cherished hallucinations) and an (over)determined poetics of exigent anxiety. Our pasts are always already present in our dreaded futures. We do not locate ourselves under these names in any aspect of tripartite time, whether sequenced or layered (as the existential dreams of zen and lyric poetry), unless of course you wish to acknowledge a certain variety of fabrication as "being in the moment".*

## VERS DORÉS  (1845)

*by Gérard de Nerval*

Eh quoi ! tout est sensible !
Pythagore.


Homme, libre penseur ! te crois-tu seul pensant
Dans ce monde où la vie éclate en toute chose ?
Des forces que tu tiens ta liberté dispose,
Mais de tous tes conseils l'univers est absent.

Respecte dans la bête un esprit agissant :
Chaque fleur est une âme à la Nature éclose ;
Un mystère d'amour dans le métal repose ;
« Tout est sensible ! » Et tout sur ton être est puissant.

Crains, dans le mur aveugle, un regard qui t'épie :
À la matière même un verbe est attaché…
Ne la fais pas servir à quelque usage impie !

Souvent dans l'être obscur habite un Dieu caché ;
Et comme un œil naissant couvert par ses paupières,
Un pur esprit s'accroît sous l'écorce des pierres !

# GOLDEN TOOTH  (2017)

*transmuted by Retorico Unentesi*

Say What!? everything is sensible!
*Pythagoras.*


Oh Man, a free thinker! So you think you're the thin
king? In this world where life bursts into everything?
Forces you fold your freedom fasts,
But consonants tease the universe in your absence.


Respect the beast in its spiral spirit agile:
Checkered flowers are the name of a Nature enclosed;
A mysterious love sleeps in the metal rose;
"Everything is sensible!" Our trout surf tones
gain entry through your percussion!


Fear is the blank wall who looks like a spy to you:
Matter is a verb and memory is your adverb...
Never serve a useless purpose in a pie!


The gods hide their obscurity in a soup vent cache;
The eye is an oily comet, covert, parsed by paupers,
A purling spirit accrues in the encore of our pairs!

from Retorico Unentesi, *Soul Roulette: Transmutations of Nerval; with Extensive Appendix. 2017.*
mOnocle-Lash Anti-Press: Roanoke, Virginia. pp. 24–25.
~_^_~_^_~_^_~_^_~_^_~_^_~_^_~_^_~_^_~_^_~_^_~_^_~_^_~_^_~_^_~_^_~_^_~_^_~_^_~_^_~_^_~

*For several decades, Jim Leftwich has been among the most active nodes in the Eternal Network –
as the author of countless books of experimental writing (cf. **Doubt**, **An Ecology**) and theory (cf.
**Rascible & Kempt**, Vols. 1–3), as publisher (cf. **Xtant**, **Juxta**, and **TLPress**), in the generation
of new forms (including the much-contested Asemic Writing and Trashpo), as organiser, and as
a prolific mail artist. He is a motivating force in the vibrant avant-garde community in Roanoke,
Virginia, where **Rêvenance** is published. Leftwich's meditation on avant-chronicling addresses
how we provide the materials for future histories; these ideas are illustrated in the accompanying
reviews of events at Roanoke's Art Rat Studios, first published in the Roanoke Post-NeoAbsurdist
zine **The InAppropriated Press**. Richards' poem, which follows, addresses the same necessity.*

## another series of love songs in another wasteland  (2017)
### *by Jim Leftwich*

Obviously diary entries, poems, improvisations and extrapolations, research notes, specula-
tions, collages of quotes and other pilfered/proliferated texts, self-skeptical meditative anxi-
eties written around the looming inevitability of an actual event, notes as guard rails, barricades and fallout shelters, anti-poems, reflections on subjective memories of collective dreams
– any of my writings, in fact, whether preliminaries or post-scripts, cannot be actual compo-
nents of actual events, now or then, past for anyone or future for everyone, they can only be a
record of myself, circling an event in words, unable to name any event myself, unable to
describe a position which is my position vis a vis any event, past or future, real or imagined,
existing in its multiplicity as from the outset experientially fictional, to whatever degree, pro-
ducing almost immediately, almost as a simultaneous parallel event, a nostalgia for itself –
offering itself, to anyone who is willing to write themselves into the record of an event, as a
presence no matter how alienated within the event as it was unfolding, as potentially a text,
several texts, one certainly prior to any actual event, as research, preparation, anxiety and
desire, one during (which will occur mostly as notes taken in the mind – remember this
sequence, remember this phrase, remember these instruments and props), and one after the
event ...which is perhaps permitted, or even desired, however weakly, by someone other than
the writer... by maybe two people other than myself, if it is even safe to assert that much –

this writing, then, as a refusal to define itself, to say, with Olson, "in this place is a poem which I have not been able to write," and to leave it at that, another series of love songs in another wasteland.

/\\/\\\\/\\/\\\\\\\\\\\\\\/\\/\\\\/\\/\\/\\/\\/\\\\////\\/\\/\\\\

### July 12 @ Art Rat

Brad Chriss and Megan Blafas-Chriss: a meat poem from Dune with Megan on bass.

Brad reads a slice of Dune: "the known universe is the most precious consciousness and its navigators." he puts some meat in his mouth and reads a little more: "that it through remains the juice warning." Megan tickles the bass and thumps a short percussive antimelody. Brad stuffs a little more meat in his mouth: "is four mela tos crout fou ex." Megan plucks a hairpin skatchbox thumb-piano shuffle in E-flat major. Brad plans the knowing messiah duplex of meat experience awakened in his mouth: "spice kn pa se so growls bort brot cattle smelling tastes tl reac nose secr ha la mertl shoh lar narrow students and their mother." the known universe spells spice as a detour from the wound of bloodlines. you are ready to eat the fight of water. arrives with knives. under the vacuum controls the carrot but cannot control the carom. weird mustard and thumping launch upon the steak.

### July 12 @ Art Rat

Mister Thursday: many exaggerated thank yous as prefatory remarks. he reads a piece of a text vaguely about maybe him thinking he's better than them while they think he shouldn't think that. maybe he's right, or would be in a Beckett play, and maybe this is a Beckett play. and maybe it's not, maybe it's something else entirely, in which case he's wrong, and they're right. he shouldn't be thinking any of this, least of all the previous sentence. a violent coughing wheezing phlegm-chewing fit seizes upon him, and he hacks a yellow soldier onto the warehouse floor. he reads a little more from the text which probably isn't a radio play by Beckett or anyone else. another choking hacking phlegm-gnawing fit is seized upon him, and he spits out another grey solider onto the surfictional tarmac. this dire scene repeats itself repeatedly. he hocks a bloody Nutcracker doll without the blood. he prepares for a final grand puking, but the bag of brown or brownish-green soldiers is ingrown to his suitcase, is tangled in the sleeve of his triangular shirtwaist waistcoat. he complains that the maneuver went much more smoothly in rehearsal, crashing through the fourth wall into the fifth estate. he empties a plastic sandwich bag onto the studio dance floor. winter soldiers the colors of a subdued rainbow spill out over a copy of Kafka's The Trial. the visual syntax is intact. the book is a deracinated anti-assemblage in which words are toy soldiers. we have our marching orders: left to right, top to bottom, through the book and out into the street.

### July 12 @ Art Rat

Tomislav Butkovic & Olchar Lindsann: squiggly soundwaves scribbled in thin air refurbish the aural purview. dusty hertzsquawk remangler. thudburping squink demuddler flanged by metamodern pingo. noise retains the syntax of a harmolodic insurgency. extrapolated throat-mappings from the Dufrêne territorial tongue and larynx training manual. historiographic letteral Oedipus, within and without you, while you are watching yourself listen in the mirrors of mostly your own mind. the corpse flickers in fragments and floats away from the shadows of its own mist-remembered breathing. to have redacted such letteral orb spider is to have felt one's mind colonized by the Situationist haruspices of everyday life. electronic gurps and burgles, crench snaggle, an almost minimalist music for pavement saw and kleenex refrigerator lawn sprinklers circling their wheelbarrows in the rain. by now you should know all of this is beautiful and courageous, and you if you are reading this should also know how to use it as a talisman and a banishing ritual. syntax = synapse. subletteral sound poetry is an isometric mnemonics.

Manifesto from *The In-Appropriated Press*, No. 9, Aug–Nov. 2017. mOnocle-Lash: Roanoke, VA. Reviews from *In-Appropriated Press*, No. 8, July–Aug. 2017. Roanoke, VA.

~^~^~^~^~^~^~^~^~^~^~^~^~^~^~^~^~^~^~^~^~^~^~^~^~^~^~^~^~^~

# The Death of a College
## In Memory of Dartington College of Arts
*by Sam Richards*

***Dartington College of Arts*** *did not need to close. Its closure was political. For details read* *Richards' book,* ***Dartington College of Arts: Learning by Doing***:
*https://www.amazon.co.uk/Dartington-College-Arts-Learning-Doing/dp/0956170544*

The students ran naked,
Absolutely naked,
From one end of the town to the other -
A revealed-all dozen
On that cold evening in December
Charging and barging through the bustling crowds
Of the Christmas street market.
The students ran naked -
Young women and men in the all together
But for a rucksack that carried their clothes
For when they finished their collaborative
Frozen streak of protest
At the coming closure
Of their college of arts.
Was it really that long ago?
Seven years and more?
Right here in this town
There were bar staff that pulled pints
And discussed Dadaism after hours,
Postmodernity (for what its worth),
Performance.

Waitresses that dashed in from their dance class,
Threw on an apron
And took your order
Gracefully.
People talking bollocks
People talking insight
Irritating and grand
Nonsense and sense
With some uncertainty
As to which was which.
Marx and Foucault
Tristram Shandy and Alfred Jarry
SHITTER! SHITTER!
And Wittgenstein the miserable git,

Is the novel dead?
Is easel painting over?
Why write a symphony?
Why close a college
Where these things mattered
Urgently
Politically?

Where that which is held in the empty hand
To speak or not speak
Is pitted against the iron pitiless will of spreadsheets
The fetid demon who hears and looks
But cannot listen or see
Always wins in the bitter end.
When performed sound and silence disappear
Into the instant past
Leaving behind no measurable value
The numbers will always crunch

In the pugilism of accountancy
With biased referees
Who see only all that never glitters
In dull columns with no breath,
Shamefully barren
In their lack of imagination.

So the college closed
In a cynical blaze of misappropriated words
Such as "relocation", "merger",
And nothing remotely like it
Has emerged on the campus
Where the earth is scorched
And the past now silent.

That act of murder,
That assassination of the innocents
Leaves our town
Gazing into the entrepreneurial swamp
Where everything sacred
Turns into smart enterprise:
Coffee shops, gift shops, tapas –
Art shop – gone
Paper shop – gone
Tourist information – gone.

The town will rise from the ashes
Now blown everywhere on the wind
No doubt
But where was once the campus
Is now the silence
Of being erased from history
Before your very eyes.

The naked students that evening in December
Were the entire tale –
Defenceless, deliberately vulnerable,
Defiant, playful,
Not really shocking –
They amused and ritually outraged
All who stood before them.
And all around them was wrapped darkly
The freezing pitiless cold night,
The watching and watchful arm of the law,
The season of ill will to all men,
And the deadening fate of their college
About to unfold in a stich-up
Spelt out in a ghastly astonishment
That never fades.

~^~^~^~^~^~^~^~^~^~^~^~^~^~^~^~^~^~^~^~^~^~^~^~^~^~^~^~^~^~

## Claire Goldberg Moses & Leslie Wahl Rabine,
### *Feminism, Socialism, and French Romanticism* (Indiana University Press, 1993)
*25-Year Late Mini-Review by Olchar E. Lindsann*

This book is essential for understanding the extensive, fertile intersection of feminism and Saint-Simonian socialism in the period of both movements' self-conscious emergence. The first half explores this intersection in great detail, both the rhetorical and ideological strategies used by French feminists and their concrete communal work and ambitious public projects. The second half comprises an anthology of stunningly radical letters and articles from the *Tribune des femmes*, the first all-female feminist newspaper in history.

The unwieldy title could easily have been shortened, for the work's treatment of Romanticism betrays an utter lack of grounding or interest in the movement (one suspects the topic was forced upon them); it focuses, weirdly, on Chateaubriand and Rousseau(?) rather than the many Romanticists who were actively engaged with the Saint-Simonian movement such as the Halévy brothers, Olindé Rodrigues, Félicien David, and Liszt. Regardless, the revealing insight it offers into the life and thought of an unfairly forgotten and still-relevant movement joining economic and gender equality makes it indispensable.

*This poem is taken from the only published work of the extremely obscure Flemish avant-garde poet Monte-Naken, '**Rimes futiles**' (Futile Rhymes), published on the Parnassian small press* **Librairie des Bibliophiles** *in 1879. His work, like most Parnassian poetry, is fiercely formal in orientation, based on virtuoso, intricate patterns of sound and laying the groundwork for the development of sound poetry at the end of the century; this translation can only partly convey this patterning, which is visible in the original.*

# Sonnet On the Tomb of a Great Desperado[16]  (1879)
by Monte-Naken

*A Edmondo Carbonero.*

*For Edmondo Carbonero.*

Etre né sans vouloir naître,
souffrir sans vouloir souffrir,
mourir sans vouloir mourir:
être homme, sans vouloir l'être.

To be born not wishing to be here,
to cry not wishing to cry,
to die not wishing to die:
to be man, not wishing such peers.

Ignorer, voulant connaître;
pleurer, espérant jouir;
ramper, croyant éblouir;
paraître, pour disparaître...

To wonder, though wishing ken clear;
to weep, though toward mirth aspired;
to cringe, seeking to inspire;
To appear, just to disappear . . .

Entre la haine et l'amour,
les sanglots et le fou rire,
haleter, — la nuit, le jour…

Hatred and love in a fight,
sobs and hysterical brays,
palpitate – the day, the night . . .

Fièvre, cauchemar, délire,
néant, farce, mauvais tour,
énigme, doute, martyre!

Nightmare, fever-dream, dismay,
Abyss, farce, hapless plight,
enigma, doubt, slain saint!

*Translated by Olchar E. Lindsann*

From Monte-Naken, *Rimes futiles.* 1879. Librairie des bibliophiles: Paris, pp. 27–28. from the Revenant Archive.

---

16 *Désespéré.*

# New from mOnocle-Lash

***Soul-roulette: Transmutations of Nerval***, *by Gérard de Nerval and Retorico Unentesi.* Experimental and 'pataphysical transductions of poetry by the early avant-gardist Gérard de Nerval, rendered by the mysterious Retorico Unentesi of the Institute for Study & Application, Kohoutenberg. Padded out with extensive front-matter by eminent dead persons and an epic appendix elaborating & tangentiating upon the seams & merging of translation & poetic creation.

***Sound Rituals***, *by Jim Leftwich & billy bob beamer.* "...an evocative apparatus that generates images in the ear and auditory revelations for the eyes. In a frequently disjointed consciousness reflective of the the exploding hybrids we all live a grand sweeping music arrives that compels us to reorient outside the delusion of self and adapt to worlds superimposed, alternatively transparent and opaque, full of sudden illumination and flittering shards fading into some nameless space only this poetry can describe. At a time when even the concept of truth seems forever elusive in this liturgy we are offered the opportunity to discover firsthand and immediately what pure unfiltered experience reveals." – Jake Berry.                                     *Forward by John M. Bennett*

## In Preparation for the mOnocle-Lash Revenants Series

The **Revenant Series** imprint publishes translations, histories, and new editions of works related to the 19th Century avant-garde, including the Romanticist, Frenetic, Occultist, Utopian Socialist, Bohemian, Parnassian, Anarchist, Decadent, and Symbolist communities.

Coming Summer 2018: ***Cinders from 'Fire and Flame'***, *by Philothée O'Neddy.* New translations from the signature 1833 collection of the Bouzingo co-founder, one of the most influential, yet forgotten, writers of the Romanticist avant-garde. An appetizer for a forthcoming full-length anthology.

***Long-Term Anthologies in Preparation:*** Estimated 2019 Release: *The Frenetic Feminine* (Anthology of Female founders of the avant-garde, c.1820–40), *Incoherent Footprints of the Rabid Black Cat* (Anthology of the Hydropathes, Incoherents, and Chat Noir groups c.1880–1900) & an anthology focusing on the role of dancing in the Romanticist Avant-Garde, c.1830–50. Estimated 2020 Release: *Tales of the Bouzingo* (Anthology of the first self-declared Avant-Garde collective, 1829–34).

***Eventual Projects under Consideration:*** Who knows what order or schedule? Vocal enthusiasm or Volunteers can affect it: Forgotten Avant-Gardists from the *Annales Romantiques* / *The Occult Avant-Garde 1830 1850* / Alphonse Karr, *Stingers from Les Guêpes* / Thomas Hood, *Poems on Poverty / The Battle of 'Hernani' / Gautier, Politics, & the Cult of Art* / etc. etc.

Jan., A.Da. 102   /   A.H. 188   /   2018 C.E.

**mOnocle-Lash Anti-Press**
**REVENANT SERIES**
monoclelash.wordpress.com
monoclelash@gmail.com

# Rêvenance

## A Zine of Hauntings from Underground Histories

Issue No. 4        July 2018 (A.Da. 102, A.H. 188)

Phœbé changée en fontaine.

## Featuring

**The Dead**: Théophile Gautier / The Princess de Salm-Dyke / Georges d'Heylli / Albert Giraud / The Grandees of Badouillery / Alexandre Privat d'Anglemont / M. Adolphe / Lucien Rigaut / A.B. / Gustave Morne

**& The Living**: Olchar E. Lindsann / Raymond E. André III

*Rêvenance* is dedicated to the forgotten or untold histories of 19th Century avant-garde and dissenting countercultures. It promotes historiography practiced as game, as activism, as transgenerational collaboration, as communal memory, which running athwart the academic, refusing to describe history as finished, which does not stand apart to observe its object from a distance, in the posture of false 'objectivity' which Power always assumes. Instead: a *committed* historiography, which does not stand outside the stream of time or apart from its object: intellectual and precise, yet ludic and multi-form, one moment manifest as an essay, the next as a poem. A historiography created *within* the utopian fringe, and for the same community, responsive to our changing conditions, needs, and desires. A historiography that *we take personally*, merging imperceptibly into experiments in daily life, social praxis, and thought.

The journal is closely integrated with the Revenant Archive of roughly 500 books, prints, manuscripts, and personal items from the 19th Century avant-garde, and much of the material is drawn from the archive's material. The journal explores forgotten and newly-discovered histories of avant-garde, radical activist, utopian, and other underground countercultures. While the primary focus is on the 19th Century, earlier and later material is also welcome, and contributions directly connecting counter-cultural movements and strategies across time are particularly encouraged. The primary goal is to explore histories, communities, and themes that are not consistently represented elsewhere. *Rêvenance* seeks to develop a community of independent DIY researchers who see historical work as part of a communal praxis directed toward contemporary and future change; it is a laboratory in which countercultural history is transmuted, reflected and disseminated in the current lifestyle, writing, music, art, and thought of present-day communities of dissent or otherness.

**Edited by Olchar E. Lindsann**
*Rights retained by translators & living writers*
All other texts in the public domain
Lindsann's translations: Creative
Commons, Non-Commercial Share-Alike;
please inform us of republications

July, A.Da. 102
A.H. 188
2018 A.D.

**mOnocle-Lash Anti-Press
Revenants Series**
monoclelash.wordpress.com
revenant-archive.blogspot.com
monoclelash@gmail.com
bouzingo.blogspot.com

Post: c/o Olchar Lindsann, Editor / 2027 Mountain View Terrace SW /
Roanoke, VA 24015 / USA (**U**nfortunate, **S**ad **A**nathema)

# CONTENTS

*All uncredited translations are by Olchar E. Lindsann.*
*Many of the source texts are available online at* gallica.bnf.fr *and/or at* archive.org.

**Cover image by Olchar E. Lindsann**, collaged from: Célestin Nanteuil, *De profondes des amours* (c.1840-50), A.B., Prado (Undated, c.1835-40), M. Adolphe, *The Infernal Gallop at St. Honoré Hall*, & Gustave Morne, *Projected* Uniform (c.1848). All constituent images are photocopied from original editions held in the Revenant Archive (not sliced up!).

**Send Submissions & Correspondence to monoclelash@gmail.com**

# Forward

Strong themes have tended to emerge when preparing *Révenance,* and in this issue the theme has culminated in a special feature dedicated to the dance subculture of the Badouillards; my hope is that readers will send me their responses to publish in upcoming issues. Future features may be devoted to topics such as gender fluidity, the Evadamistes, poverty & class, racial struggles, the Kabbala & gematria in the avant-garde, and an inquest on Gautier. Interwoven with the offerings in the feature is a secondary thread, tying the neologisms and ludic language of the 19th Century avant-garde to the dance-club subculture that brought industrial workers and students into direct fellowship; and looping through it all a surprising further complication in the fraught confusion over the the taxonomy of the various microcultures of the Parisian underground in the 1830s and of the first self-identified avant-garde collectives – topped off with some glances at the feminist struggle in the wakes of three French revolutions (1789, 1830, and 1848).

## *Special Feature: A Partymar With the Badouillards!*

This special feature developed rather jaggedly as I followed up an increasingly intriguing, yet also ambivalent, micro-culture called the Badouillards [pronounce: Bad-we-are's – a rather delightful homophone!] that flourished for about twenty years, from 1830-1850. Imagine a combination of Rave/danceclub culture, an anarchist squat, and a Frat House, then place it in 1830s Paris . . . Rather than present a unified history, I determined to present a selection of primary texts that display both its promising and its seamy sides, in the hope of provoking some reader/s to offer their own reactions and interpretations in future issues (*hint–!*)

My interest (read: knowledge) in the Badouillards stemmed from Enid Starkie's account of them in her biography of Petrus Borel, after which I was left to exclusively 19th century french sources. Increasingly, I find that the Parisian dance-club scene was as important a catalyst and mixing-ground of avant-garde, working-class, and student subcultures in the 19th Century undergrounds as jazz, punk, free improv, noise, etc. have been to the 20th Century and contemporary undergrounds. In both cases, the results can be both exhilarating and problematic.

What is there to learn from the Badouillards today? Anything? You tell me.

~^~^~^~^~^~^~^~^~^~^~^~^~^~^~^~^~^~^~^~^~^~^~^~^~^~^~

*The first record of the Badouillards was instigated when almost the whole group was arrested at the big public Carnival Ball in 1833 for dancing the cancan (illegal for licentiousness) and then rioting against the cops. This is the newspaper article on the incident and trial, from the **Gazette des Tribunaux**, which printed reports and transcriptions of court cases. Note that the article leads with the description of their collectivist, proto-anarchist ethos, which may give the clue to the real reason for the arrest; Paris was currently in the grips of a "Red Scare" in the Saint-Simonist movement.*

# The Badouillards on Trial  (1833)

– Do you know what the society of *Badouillards* is? If we are to believe the explanations of Mr. Chicaoisneau, lawyer for several of the accused who, a dozen of them, were arrested in the course of the last month at the Pantheon's masked ball, the spirit of socialism[1] and saint-simonian promiscuity[2] exists among the *Badouillards*. Money, pains, pleasures, studies, grisettes,[3] books, finery, boots and opinions, everything is communal among the Badouillards. The Badouillard, a collective entity composed of a score of students, took a fancy, in the month indicated, to go to the Pantheon ball. The Badouillard was disguised as a mattress, a costume absolutely all the rage, and spent sixty francs for twenty sets of mattress-ticking. The Badouillard donned his twenty costumes, made an entrance like that of forty and noise like a hundred; they soon got warmed up, and little by little worked their way up from the *cancan* to the immoral vices of the *chahut*. The city police, another collective entity, composed of only four individuals, was called for; he took the most civil reprimands as threats, and they ended up collaring one out of twenty Badouillards. The others who were compelled to demand, in accordance with the Badouillard

---

1 *Association*, the favoured word until mid-century when *socialisme* became the predominant tag.

2 The socialist-feminist movement of Saint-Simonism was at its peak, and their espousal of (theoretically) non-patriarchal polygamy was being used by the government to end public support in the press, and to legally shut down their commune, newspapers, soup kitchens and free schools. The communal property of the group suggests socialist influences, or ay least excuses, while their behaviour is closer to the frenetic Romanticism of the time or later forms of anarchism. Other documents put a more misogynist light on the sexual dynamic of the group, which did however admit women as full members–upon special conditions.

3 Unmarried working-class girls, presumably in this case the female members, "badouillardes".

117

charter, solidarity in the slammer or in freedom, rushed as a single man upon the police, who were forced to give way to numbers, beat a hasty retreat and give up the prisoners. But the police's withdrawal was merely a prudent step; soon he returned stronger and more numerous, and as the Badouillard carried this night his name spelled out upon twenty hats, it was an easy thing to recognise the delinquents, whose exultation could be subdued at leisure under the influence of violin next door and the flimsy costume that they were carrying all the while.

In short the entire offense can be summed up as a few wallops, a few very hurtful epithets, gestures supporting, less than anywhere else, due to the make-up of the ball,[4] the character of public immorality. It seems, in fact, that the fairer sex who embellish our existence as well as the masked balls of the Saint-Benoît cloister, are composed for the most part, these days, of smooth-faced scholars dressed as marquessas, maids, fisherwomen, etc., etc. Keeping in mind that at the same time, authority has thrown a veil of forgetfulness over the grand Opera's costume balls, in which several distinguished figures were, they say, arrested under the troublemakers' mask, one might think that there would likewise have been indulgence and forgetfulness, due to the carnival's jubilation, in favour of the overly-reckless Badouillard. It was not so, and a dozen students were brought before the 6th district [court] today.

In their argument, the defendants alleged in their defense that they had until then played around at the Pantheon's masked ball with the most unlimited freedom, that they did not dance *the chahut,* but a perfected *cancan,* and that moreover the excesses of the carnival temporarily tossed a veil over the severity of articles 330 and 224 of the penal Code, which punishes outrages against public morality and resisting arrest, and gave at the same time new vigour to the article 463 of the same Code which admits, in favour of delinquents, attenuating circumstances.

Four of the defendants were acquitted, and the rest most guilty condemned to several days in prison.

From the *Gazette des Tribunaux*, No. 2343. Sunday, 17 février 1833.

~^~^~^~^~^~^~^~^~^~^~^~^~^~^~^~^~^~^~^~^~^~^~^~^~^~^~^~^~^~^~^~

---

4 Probably referring to the balls involving working and lower-middle-class people, considered by the bourgeoisie to be more easily swayed by immorality.

*If the 1833 article makes the group sound like an anarchist squat, parts of their official charter are more sickeningly reminiscent of a Frat House. (Variant reading, anyone?) There are two published versions; the 1838 version had probably been in place in some form since 1833. The second version was published in 1844, and while a bit more verbally playful, it is also noticeably more misogynist. This is the 1844 version, with variations from the earlier text marked in the footnotes along with cross-references to Rigaut's* **Dictionary of Slang** *(see next entry).*

# The Magna Carta of Badouillards (1838 & 1844)

## Based upon the Magna Carta[5] of the Great Britain, by the Grandees of Badouillery.

Temperance is the death of societies which badouillent.[6]

Badouillerie is the death of temperance societies.

Between badouillerie and temperance is the proper realm of wisdom.

Wisdom is the entirety of virtues, each of which becomes a vice at the carnival.

We, the very select and venerable fathers of badouillardery, to all partiers, gobblers, cancan-ers, cachucha-ers, varsovienn-ers,[7] ballgoers, superballgoers, rigadooners and rigadoonesses,[8] greetings; by this epistle and without preamble, be it known that we have granted ourselves and do grant ourselves the charter of which the articles follow:[9]

---

5 *Grande Charte.* Literally Great Charter, but I have substituted the accepted English name (albeit imported from Latin) for the document. The parody runs no deeper than the title.

6 "To rush to the public dances, the places of debauchery" – Rigaut's *Dictionary of Parisian Slang* (see notes in following article).

7 The cancan, caichucha (or cauchuc, etc.), and varsovienne were popular dances; the former two were legally banned as indecent, and the Badouillards had been subjected to mass arrests for dancing them; the latter was a very recently-imported dance from Poland.

8 The rigadoon was another popular dance.

9 The 1838 version reads: "We, the very select and venerable fathers of badouillardierie, to all partiers, gobblers, cancan-ers, cachucha-ers, ballgoers, superballgoers: greetings, cancan without fiddle; good wine without hangover; love without remorse. Make it known, have granted ourselves and do grant ourselves the following charter:"

119

*Art. 1st*. All badouillards of the same size and capacity are equal before the party;[10]

*Art. 2.* Every badouillard who, when entering the ball, is not already cock-eyed and ambling in zig-zags shall be deprived of his civil rights;

*Art. 3.* The Society of Badouillards alone enjoys the right to amuse itself at the ball and to prevent others from amusing themselves;[11]

*Art. 4.* One cannot be received in badouillardery, if they have had the misfortune to remain in possession of their balance for two Sundays in a row.

*Art. 5.* Any applicant who shall not be drunk at least fifty-two times throughout the year shall not be admitted. Sunday and Monday only count as one.[12]

*Art. 6.* Women married or not shall only be affiliated with the society under the following conditions;[13]

*Art. 7.* The badouillardess[14] shall not be forced to exhibit a certificate of good life and manners. She will on the contrary need to produce a statement which proves that she parties with the first comer. This obligatory statement must be signed by at least six members;[15]

*Art. 8.* She will have to have woken up at least twenty times outside of her bed, without knowing by whom she has been stripped and laid, and have regained the exercise of her functions with neither heartache nor migraine;

*Art. 9.* The Badouillardess, at the time of her application, must bring a certificate certifying that she has been vaccinated with a quality vaccine or that she has at least had smallpox once;

*Art. 10.* Every Badouillardess must submit to a visit which will prove to the assembled society that that, from head to foot, she is exempt from every flaw and infirmity…;

*Art. 11.* Feeble physiques will not be rejected; but they will be put to the test: there are proud partiers who seem as if they only have one breath of life, and who work it no less joyfully for the

---

10 In the 1838, there was no provision for differing size and capacity.

11 In 1838, they were allowed to amuse themselves, but preventing others' fun was not mandated.

12 Conditions 4 and 5 do not appear in the 1838 charter.

13 Only articles 7-10 relate specifically to female members. In the 1838 version, numbers 7, 9 and 10 were numbered separately under the subheading "Conditions for Admission of the Ladies." The aggressively misogynist clause 8 was added in 1844.

14 *Badouillarde.* The terminal "e" signifies a female Badouillard, here and throughout.

15 Only the first sentence was in the 1838 version.

common good;[16]

*Art. 12.* The *cancan* is generally recognised as the dance of badouillards who must set themselves to embellishing it. The varsovienne and the cachuca are permitted in certain exceptions by the band at the Taglioni.[17] The cahut, which is the cachuca of the thug[18] and his thugess or thugette,[19] shall not be tolerated, save on permission of the gentleman of the police, at mardi gras and the third Thursday of Lent.[20]

*Art. 13.* The badouillards of every sex and every age must mutually support each other in quarrels and beatings, and receive punches for each other, if it comes to that;

*Art. 14.* They must contribute all of their alcoholic and muscular aptitude to the glory of the society and to the fame of its general staff.[21]

*Art. 15.* Any badouillard or badouillardess who is not at the Titus[22] must be excessively disheveled;

*Art. 16.* The worn-out shoes and pierced-through stockings, the muddy skirt's measurements, the waist without corset, the dress slipping off a shoulder and the shawl[23] dragging in the stream are the badouillardess's image. Her hat, in case she should own one, should be carabossed[24] like an old tin saucepan, having made for thirty years the coffee and cabbage soup of a decrepid con-

---

16 Not included in the earlier version.

17 One of the most popular permanent dance clubs in Paris, run by a family of prominent dancers.

18 *Voyou.* According to Rigaut's *Dictionnaire,* a poorly education alcoholic, and/or a criminal street urchin (he gives Hugo's character of Gavroche as an example; Dickens' Artful Dodger is an English equivalent).

19 *Son voyelle ou voyouse.* An untranslatable pun, literally "his vowel or thugette". The joke is that there are two ways one could feminize the masculine *Voyou* (see previous note), one of which would result in the word "Voel" (*Voyelle*).

20 The 1838 version listed only the cancan.

21 The 1838 version had been more communal: "...shall contribute all their power to the glory of the society and to the fame of its collective name." That version ended with this commandment; numbers 15-17 and the verses were added in 1844.

22 Presumably a dance club.

23 *Schall.* At this time, a recently-introduced garment still associated with Orientalism. According to the 1828 Boniface *Dictionnaire Français-Anglais et Anglais-Française,* Librairie classique-élélmentaire et catholique: Paris – "A long piece of silken or woolen material, which the inhabitants of Egypt wind around their head. The shawl is being adapted by the french ladies, who wear it on their shoulders."

24 *Carabossé,* "wicked fairy godmother" (n.) is the only definition I can find, but it seems to be used here as a (presumably lost slang) adjective drawn from a verb.

vent-porter. The badouillard goes without cravat; he suspends his trousers by a single strap, whose sinking belt gives the shivers to morality . . . His tinplate or silk must be unprocessed in order to be less casual; A long frock-coat open in the back is his most typically distinctive mark;

*Art. 17.* The eye poached with black-butter-sauce[25] shall be considered an adornment; with two black eyes, the badouillard will be worshipped like an Apollo and the badouillardess as a Venus.

Given in our Orgy palace in continued progress:
Day and year, which need fold nevermore,[26]
On January fifth Eighteen fourty-four,
At three in the morning, having strong wine imbued,
Blue, white, red, black, with which we are infused,
Amidst all girths and sizes of pints and of flasks,
Sealed on the brown bottom of our emptied casks,
Before heading out, to aimlessly wander,
Toward that to which each boozer sadly surrenders.

*Signed*, the President of the United Badouillards,

Of Hog-in-Sowe;[27]

By certified copy, the Secretary,

Francis Drink-Always, known as Sleazeball-of-Rum[28]

1838 version from *Physiologie de l'Opéra, du Carnaval, du Cancan et de la Cachucha, par un vilain masque.* Dessins de Henri Emy, Raymond-Bocquet Éditeur, Paris 1842, pages 47-49.

1844 version from *Catéchisme du Carnaval ou l'art de se dire de gros mots sans se fâcher ni fâcher personne ; répertoire de gaité à l'usage des amis de la joie ; par le secrétaire perpétuel de l'Académie des Badouillards, Flambards, Chicards, Braillards et autres Sociétés buvantes.*, B. Renaud, éditeur, Paris 1844⁶, pages 24 à 29.

---

25 *L'oeil poché au beurre noir.* "Poached eye" is the french equivalent of "black eye" (translated thus in the following clause), hence the rather grotesque breakfast metaphor; direct or indirect echoes of Romanticism here, via the evocation of Rabelais …

26 *Jour et an, dont il ne faut rien rabattre*

27 *Porc-en-Truye.* I take this as a play on *Porc-en-Truie*, "Hog-and-Sow", probably reflecting Parisian pronunciation or dialect.

28 *Francis Boit-Toujours, dit Poliçon-de-Rhum*

UN GALOP INFERNAL À LA SALLE S.<sup>t</sup> HONORÉ.

**An Infernal Gallop at St. Honoré Hall.** by M. Adolphe. (Undated, c. 1835-45) *Dances themselves could become violent in the 1830s and '40s; seen here is one of the most violent: the* **Infernal Galop***, in which pairs of dancers rushed around at top-speed, trampling whomever fell (as seen here) – essentially identical to a punk circle-pit 150 years later; it was often accompanied by pistol-shots fired in time. It was the favourite dance of the ultra-Romanticist, Jeune-France and Bousingot subcultures.* from the collection of the Revenant Archive.

~^~^~^~^~^~^~^~^~^~^~^~^~^~^~^~^~^~^~^~^~^~^~^~^~^~^~^~^~

# From the Jeune-France to the Badouillards: A Journey thru Slang

*The initial genesis of this special feature was lexicographic: the Badouillards had some very interesting linguistic practices, as we find here. From those practices, new sources led me unexpectedly to the old (for me) question of the naming of early avant-garde collectives, and thence to the other materials.*

*This section combines two documents: one in the main text, and the other in the footnotes. In the process it both clarifies how thoroughly integrated the Romanticist avant-garde was with dance-club culture, and complicates the already bewildering issue of the naming of the first self-described "avant-garde" collective, known variously as the Petit-Cénacle, Jeunes-France, and Bouzingo. We should not be surprised at this confusion, because Parisian underground subculture in the 1830s-40s had just as many evolving, merging, passing scenes, micro-genres, fads, etc. as today, and borders were rarely clear or long-standing.*

*The main text is from an article on their development by Privat-d'Anglemont, a tireless chronicler of the Paris underground. It first discusses a broad, vague youth subculture labelled by the press as "Jeune-France". [Pronounce: June-Fronce] This is not the avant-garde Romanticist group, but rather the avant-group was* **labeled** *by the press as a symbol/figurehead* **of** *this scene (hence they fucked with the spelling to call themselves the Jeunes-France). Likewise, it discusses the evolution to the broad, vague youth subcultures* **labeled** *by the press as "Bousingots" [pronounce: Booze-on-joe]. Again, the* **same** *avant-garde group was then labeled by the press as a symbol/figurehead of this new scene (hence they* **again** *fucked with the spelling to temporarily rename themselves the "Bouzingos").*

*Enter the Badouillards! The bulk of the article focuses on their slang, where the influence of underground Romanticism is very clear. Much of the slang persisted long enough to end up in Lucien Rigaut's* **Dictionary of Parisian Argot** *fifty years later, printed by the publisher of the Chat Noir, Incoherents, and Hydrophathes groups (see Rêvenance #1). Below are his definitions of Badouillards, while his entries of the rest of the words Privat d'Anglemont discusses are cross-referenced in the footnotes.*

~~~~~~~~~~~~~~~~~~~~~~~~

## Two Definitions
from Lucien Rigaut, *Dictionnaire d'argot moderne*. 1888. 2nd Edition. Paul Ollendorff: Paris.

***Badouillard.*** Partier, epicurian, boon companion of pleasures, good cheer, and public balls. The Baouillard, one of numerous incarnations of the Bousingot, blossomed from 1840 to 1850.[29] The society of Badouillards was, on principle, composed of students. In order to be counted among this society, he must submit honourably to certain trials. There was that of dining, of the ingurgitation of champagne, punch and strong liquors, of telling-off, of the duel, of nights passed, of the ball. Those who emerged triumphant from these trials, whose

---

29 This contradicts Privat d'Anglemont, but is much better supported than his assertions by documentary evidence.

health and sometimes reason were at stake, were then proclaimed "Badouillard." – "The vestibule of the opera was overrun by a host of charming drainage traps,[30] delicious Badouillards." (Musée Philipon, The Masked Balls.) – "Great Charter of the Badouillards. Art. 2. – Every badouillard who is not drunk when entering the ball, shall be deprived of his civil rights." (Physiologie du Carnival, 1842.)

*Badouillarde*. Female of badouillard species.[31] "Every Badouillarde must prove to the society that, from head to toe, she does not possess any infirmity." (Physiologie du Carnival, 1842.)

# A Subcultural Historico-etymology by Privat d'Anglemont (1854)

[The Bousingos][32] likewise fully adopted an interesting manner, the visage pale and the eyes sombre, especially following the success of *Anthony* and *Angèle*;[33] they had nothing against carrying a dagger and death's head in their pocket, with clothing sombre in colour, the face of someone disinherited and wretched hair. But it didn't suit them to hook themselves up with a hair shirt and kneel for hours on end upon clammy flagstones of gothic naves. The Bousingots, a bit more sober in their literary and artistic theories, whilst preserving their hair worn long à la Buridan[34] or cropped short à la the *rebel*, swung their thurible to the side of beauty, youth, wine and beer. They turned into *partiers*, *materialists*, and, in order to characterise this twenty-first incarna-

---

30 *Cureur d'égout*. Apparently an untranslatable pun: technically "drainage cleaner/curer", but homonymically *Coureur de gout*, which is literally "runner of taste" but in slang would signify "fortune hunters / womanizers of taste".

31 The dictionary uses *femelle*, the form of female usually reserved for biological texts.

32 Privat d'Anglemont here refers to the underground youth subculture of militant, romanticist, neo-Jacobin socialism, not the specific avant-garde group known by that name, who were branded thus by the press and who, when they eventually used the name themselves, détourned the spelling to *Bouzingo* to distinguish themselves from the broader movement. (Petrus Borel and Philothée O'Neddy, however, were both simultaneously *Bouzingos* and prominent *bousingots*.) Anglemont is tracing the evolution of micro-cultures within avant-garde Romanticism between 1830 and around 1840; the period he is describing in this excerpt seems to be approximately 1833-36. Rigaud's *Dictionnaire d'argot moderne*, 1888, Olendorff:Paris, places them later, from 1840-50. (p.22)

33 Romanticist dramas by Alexandre Dumas, in 1831 and 1833 respectively, at which the Parisian underground struggled in the audience against Classicist reactionaries.

34 Medieval secular philosopher.

A.B., **Prado**. (Undated, c. 1835-40) *The unidentified artist of this print celebrated one of the first pubs where (as careful scrutiny of the iconography suggests) the arts, political revolution, debauchery, medievalist cos-play, and friendship were fused into Bohemian subculture.* Revenant Archive.

tion [of underground counterculture], took the noble name of *Badouillards*[35].

With each incarnation, the style changed, the spirit was one with the situation. The badouillards were the first to set fire to what they had once loved: they became the irreconcilable enemies of the medieval period and its jargon. They discovered the absurd aspect of today's lifestyle. Everything became *of Toledo*, even beefsteak and potatoes.[36] "Give me some cheese from Brie, but from Brie-of-Toledo." The words *good, excellent, exquisite, wonderful,* etc. were replaced in the new lexicon by these two words: *of Toledo*.

As for the rest of the language, they limited themselves to slicing off the final consonant, so as to substitute the syllable *mar*. They said

---

35 According to Rigaut's *Dictionnaire,* the root word is the Parisian slang term *Badouiller,* "to rush to the public dances, the places of debauchery – in the jargon of partiers of twenty-one years." We also find here *Badouille,* "Man who, in his household, owns no trousers except by name." p. 23.

36 One does indeed see this phrase pop up in a few satires of Parisian subculture around 1833. Its meaning and derivation from the theatre are also reflected in Rigaut's *Dictionnaire,* where it is tied explicitly to Romanticist subculture and went out of usage as Romanticism declined. Rigaud adds that it was usually coupled with the word "good".

*grocemar* for *grocer*, *bakemar* for *baker*, *cafemar* for *café.*[37] And so on. Such was the spirit of the time. It's true that our fathers were all convulsed with laughter at putting the word *turlurette*[38] at the end of each couplet of a song, and we ourselves have long amused ourselves with that so well-known refrain *la rifla, fla, fla*, etc. What does MAR signify? Precisely the same thing as *la rifla, la, la*. No one can ever know.[39]

As for the *Badouillards'* lifestyle, they differed from those of *Jeune-France*. For to be a good *Badouillard*, he must pass three or four nights at the ball, dine all day and dash in costume and mask into every café in the latin quarter until midnight, opening-time of the Variétés, Palais-Royal, and Musard balls.[40] This they called happiness. This went on until 1838, at which point the fantasist school absorbed Jeune France and Badouillards.[41]

from Alexandre Privat d'Anglemont, *Paris Anecdote.* Undated (1854). A. Delahays: Paris. pp 189-91.
from the collection of the Revenant Archive.

37 According to Rigaut: "**Mar.** Slangish flexional ending. *Wigmakemar*, wigmaker; *policimar*, policeman; *shopkeepemar,*shopkeeper. Most of the grandma words ("mots de la langue régulaière") which have no eqivalent in slang, are formed by means of the flexional ending *mar*, the rest by means of the flexionals *much* or *mince*.

38 This word does not appear in Rigaut's dictionary, but has a long and irregular history as a slang term. Originally very obscure medieval stringed instrument, known in both English and french as a *vielle* or, even less commonly, a *turlurette* or *tureluette*. The word appears as *turluette* from the 12th Century, and in this form in the mid-15th Century, now signifying not the instrument but the refrain of the song played on it, a century later as slang for a 'party girl'. It then disappears until revived in the 1820s with the non-semantic usage described by Privat d'Anglemont in the main text (it is referred to as onomatopoeia), as evidenced by the Romanticist popular poet Béranger in 1829. By the 1850s we find the word again meaning 'party-girl' or *grisette* as well as a non-semantic word interjected "to spice up conversation". For etymology, see entries for "turlurette" in CNRTL, http://www.cnrtl.fr . For the vielle/turlurette, see https://www.commeunefleche.com/instrument-de-musique-en-6-lettres/

39 Contemporary hip hop offers a strong contemporary example of the same phenomenon: *diggity, schn-, -izzle*, etc.

40 Three of the most massive public dance seasons in Paris, mostly durning the winter Carnival, but periodically throughout the year and, by the end of the 1830s, in permanent dancehalls including Musard's.

41 Clearly not entirely, as the 1844 Badouillard charter shows.

*The previous article suggests that the intense language-play of the avant-garde Jeunes-France/Bouzingo group, particularly their development of a system of slang ("Romanticist Argot" so dense that even moderate Romantics found it impossible to understand their conversations with each other, might owe a good deal to their documented immersion in dance culture and the access onto less-regulated working-class uses of language. This 1877 article from Heylli's historiographic proto-Zine (an inspiration for* **Révenance***) about literary neologisms turns up several surprising ones, including a number attributed to the Jeunes-France co-founder Gautier (see the following sonnet and his sonnet in the previous issue). My lexicographic sources for my notes include the 11 editions of 4 dictionaries published between 1694 and 1935 cross-referenced on the amazing* Dictionnaires d;autrefois *project (https://artfl-project.uchicago.edu/content/dictionnaires-dautrefois), plus the 1828 Boniface Dictionary, Rigaut's dictionary cited in the previous article, wordreference.com, wiktionary, & other online sources.*

# Some Neologisms (1877)

*by Georges d'Heylli*

—*Some Neologisms.* The *Event*[42] offered up, some time ago, a very engaging article on the subject of neologisms thought up by our most illustrious authors and of the fate that they have had in our everyday language, where some even ended up being admitted. Here is a rather interesting list of those to whom all later right to quote was refused apart from the book and the writer who had first published them.

I was born savage and not *shameridden* (Chateaubriand).[43]

Ferrare is almost *inhabitual*[44], otherwise put, to replace the word *desert*.

Michelet devised the adjectives *ensavaged*[45], *enshadowed*;[46] Gautier spoke of the *dermissed*[47]

---

42 *L'Événement* was a centre-left newspaper published in Paris.

43 This word, *vergogneux,* seems to mean "shameful", which there's a word for already: *honteux.* What is the nuance Chateaubriand (the Christian Romanticist novelist & politician) was playing on?

44 *Déshabitée.* Now included in the dictionary, "not according to habit", but seldom used; I have attempted to defamiliarize the word in translation. The word appears in Chateaubriand's *Memories From Beyond the Grave (mémoirs d'outre-tombe)*

45 *Ensauvagé* Now included in the dictionary as a past participle of the verb "ensavager", "to make savage". Michelet was a Liberal Romanticist historian and novelist, one of the major figures of 19th Century French historiography.

46 *enténébré.* Now in the dictionary as a past participle of *entenebrer*, "to envelop in shadow"

47 *Peaussu.* I hypothesize that the word is formed of "skin" (peau) treated as a verb and conjugated in

brow of an old man; Souvestre thought up *sleepified*[48] hearts, figures which are *reliefed*[49] in a semi-light and also the *withering;*[50] Proudhon expounded on the *in-self*[51] of things. It is also Th. Gautier who thought up *mannerism,*[52] *modernity*[53] and *afterfruits*[54] as opposed to firstfruits. Mr Thiers himself, in his *History of the Consulate and Empire,* spoke of the *invincibility*[55] of his heroes; he also created the word *indemonstratable*[56]; finally, in order to distinguish soldiers in state of punishment from those placed in the grip of the recruitment law, he invented two expressions as concise as they are picturesque: punishmenteers[57] and namables[58]. Arsène Houssaye[59] spoke to us of the *unworry*[60] of Fontenelle; Stendhal talked about *disinterest;*[61] Gonzalès, of *languid*[62] glances; Mazères, of

the passé simple, then applied like a participle. A rather circuitous guess, so I'm open to better ones. There are several extant french words for "skinned," but this is not among them. I have attempted to maintain the unfamiliarity of the word in translation. Gautier, a key member of the Jeunes-France / Bouzingo group, had a tremendous influence on the first four generations of the avant-garde, as poet and as mentor (see his poem following this article).

48 *Torpéfiés.* Conjectural; I'm guessing at "torpeur" or drowsiness as a root...?

49 *Relieffaient* = "put into relief", i.e. against the soft light; again, I have translated to recover a degree of unfamiliarity to the word.

50 *Flétrissement* is now in the dictionary.

51 *En-soi,* an important term in Proudhon's Anarchist theory.

52 *Maniérisme.* Now in the dictionary; It is unclear whether Gautier coined the term in its art-historical sense (as art critic) or its behavioral sense (as a dandy and novelist).

53 *Modernité.* Also now in common parlance, of course; interesting to see the word attributed to the most influential avant-gardist of the first half of the 19th Century.

54 Untranslatable, because there is no single english word for French *primeurs,* or early spring vegetables. Théo's *Postmeurs* would be the dregs of the harvest, with a single word changing only its prefix.

55 *Invincibilité.* Now in the dictionary.

56 *Indémontrable.* Still not in standard dictionaries.

57 *Punitionnaire* had in fact appeared in the *Littré* dictionary a few years earlier, in 1873. French Wiktionary cites that volume, but lists the etymology as unknown and solicits information. Anyone want to help me figure out how to use a wiki in french to add it? (en.wiktionary doesn't contain it.)

58 *Appelables.* Indeed, this word seems not to exist as a noun in French (though the singular form exists as an adjective).

59 Member of the Bohême Doyenné group, acolyte of Gautier, editor of the avant-garde journal *l'Artiste,* but then director of the Imperial Opera under Napoleon III.

60 Now an accepted word, *Insouci.*

61 Also incorporated into the dictionaries, *Désintérêt.*

62 Languide has since been accepted as a word.

*mockable*[63] sensitivities; Eugène Sue, of *fluctioned*[64] games. Finally the author of this summary closes by proposing a neologism of his own fashioning, and here's the prickly closing of his article:

"When one announces snow one says: The snow should be expected.

Why not: A snowed should be expected?

Send back the *sinecurists*[65] (hey! another one!) of the Academy Dictionary."

– from *Gazette Anecdotique Littéraire, Artistique et Bibliographique.* Year 2, No. 6, March 31, 1877. ed. Georges d'Heylli. Libraire des bibliophiles: Paris. pp 184–185. *Collection of the Revenant Archive.*
~^~^~^~^~^~^~^~^~^~^~^~^~^~^~^~^~^~^~^~^~^~^~^~^~^~^~^~^~

*Gautier ends up in this journal a lot, and he always provokes long, contentious introductions by the editor. This is because he played a central role in underground, experimental culture for over 40 years, and his influence on the literary avant-garde was both profound and problematic – so much that he was almost systematically erased from the avant-garde 's collective consciousness by the Surrealists. Yet he is ignored to our peril. The problem: he has been enshrined (especially in anglophone criticism) as the father of de-politicized, "Art for Art's Sake" (a term he tossed out when describing what he called the 'cult of art' in his massively influential* **Preface to Mlle. de Maupin**). *Gautier truly does have much to answer for here – in retrospect, we can see how he set a politically distanced pattern that was not shaken free of until the Modernists. However, when read carefully and outside of Walter Pater's critical shadow, even his famous* **Preface** *turns out much more nuanced and complex, if still flawed. I would propose (some other time) that the vision he proposes there is as close to Hakim Bey's Ontological Anarchy as Pater's Art for Art's Sake. In fact, he specifically* **espouses** *Fourierist socialism in that tract, giving the very same reasons that the Surrealists and Situationists would later offer. What he renounces is his belief in the "political" electoral plane as an effective vehicle for change. This poem from his 1st collection, is explicitly political and calls out the current "Liberal Monarchy" that took over after the July Revolution of 1830, the year of publication, and its suppression of multiple democratic uprisings in its wake. Four years later, in the* **Maupin** *Preface, he echoed the poem's point: "What matters it whether 'tis a sword, a holy-water sprinkler, or an [bourgeois-republican] umbrella that rules you? It's a stick all the same... it would be far more progressive... to break it and throw away the pieces." In experimental fashion, even his syntax fractures here, along with his faith in positivist revolution. (Thanks to K. Ladenheim for translation advice!)*

---

63 *Moquables.* Also in the dictionary now, and traced to the seventeenth century, long before used by the popular Franco-Haitian playwright Edouard Mazarès.

64 *Fluctionée.* (Sue used the infinitive.) *Fluctionner* is a truly obscure word, apparently appearing only in his play and a handful of medical texts from the 1840s, in which it is given as a synonym for *frictionner,* to rub…. I have maintained the root and simply anglified the suffix.

65 *Sinécuristes.* Now a french word, though rare: One with an easy job that's a glorified handout for an untalented hack, like Poet Laureate.

# Sonnet VII (1830)

## by *Théophile Gautier*

> Liberty of July! Woman of bust divine,
> And whose body ends in a tail!
> Gérard de Nerval

> And this blind life of theirs is so debased,
> They envious are of every other fate.
> *Inferno, canto III*

With this disgraceful age tis high time that we break it;
The fatal finger placed upon its brow condemned[66]
As upon hell's gates: Hope depleted! – Friends,
Enemies, public, kings, all trump us taken in.

A budget elephant sucks gold by trunk taken in;
In their thrones yet a-quake from yesterday's ascents,
From kinsmen overthrown they keep all, but rescind
The palm prompt with gifts and pomp breathtaking.

And yet in July, neath the sky's indigo,
There where the cobbles lurched,[67] they proffered promises
Equal to Charles tenth's overseen masses!

Alone, Poetry manifest in Hugo
Refused deluding us, of which palms divine
Enshadow our debris, destiny inclined.

— *Trans. Olchar E. Lindsann*

from Théophile Gautier, *Poésies Complètes, Tome premier.* 1884. Charpentier: Paris. p.107.

---

66 In the original, this line ends with *a mis*, "placed", which is an exact homophone of *amis*, "friends", in the next line. I have found it impossible to translate this wordplay.
67 Referring to the paving-stones of Paris being pried up to build barricades, a potent symbol of revolution in France throughout the 19th Century.

***Translator's Introduction***: *The Arts are inseparable from the phenomenon of synaesthesia. For all who drink deeply at the fount of the muses, the many streams flow into one great over-arching flood of sensation. Images can have a smell, music a color, and so forth. This phenomenon can develop even more deeply into moral and aesthetic metaphors; the more one allows oneself to dwell in such reveries. Here then, is the impression (as our old friend Albert Giraud describes) that a waltz by Chopin leaves upon the sensibilities of our old, heartbroken 'son of the moon', Pierrot…*

# Chopin's Waltz (1884)

### *by Albert Giraud*

Like spit with blood imbued,
From the mouth of a consumptive falling,
This music still is calling
With morbid, mournful mood.

A red sound – within a white dream
Pale gown with scarlet galling
Like spit with blood imbued,
From the mouth of a consumptive falling

Soft theme, violently hued;
This waltz melancholic
Infuses with a physical flavor;
Disturbing aftertaste I savor,
Like spit with blood imbued.

*– Translated by Raymond E. André III.*

from Albert Giraud, *Pierrot Lunaire: Rondels Bergamasques*, 1884.

# TWO POEMS

## by Constance Marie Theis, the Princess De Salm

*Constance Marie Theis was a leading feminist intellectual and poet first living in Germany as an expatriate from Napoleon's regime, then in Paris during the first growing ferment of Romanticism. She was born into the lower aristocracy; the revolution disinherited her family, but did allow her to legal divorce her husband (a hernia surgeon) and marry the German Count of Salm-Dyck, apparently for love. Although she publicly distanced her work from Romanticism and seems to have been ambivalently liberal, she was a friend of Madame de Staël and her weekly salon in Paris was an important early meeting-point for the early liberal French romantics such as Stendhal, Chenier, Vernet, and Dumas as well as the Marquis de Lafayette and the polymath philosopher Humboldt – while this very poem was published in the 1829 **Annales Romantiques (Romanticist Chronicles)** anthology.*

## The Blindness of the Century (1828)

Always the passions, human infirmities,
Have lain to waste the earth, prolonging enmities;
But within the excess of this vast turmoil
An other nature is proclaiming other ills.
Dare we declare: All is begun and is done;
The haughty oak's duration sap outruns;
The opened fruit, dropped down, offers up unto our gaze
Only germs of fruits to bloom in future days.
Man too, in epochs when he endures outrage,
Sees, in his ripened sons, re-emerge another age.
Why couldn't the nations, the peoples, the states,
In this circuit infinite etern'ly circulate?
These thrones that the age erects and topples over;
This derelict Greece and who climbs from its cinders;
These empires mighty have already long flown,
Others already shine and until now unknown;
Does it not confirm that unyielding rules
Conduct the universe with kindred tools?

133

# A Burn
## On Female Writers (1798)

What woe for the female writer!
Just heavens! vocation forlorn!
Whether she be loved or feared,
One and all shall put her down.

If she's simple and too austere,
'Tis, they say, *pretentiousness!*
Should she savour one second of fun,
*An exhibitionist,* they declare;
Anything she dares allow herself
Some kind of sin they read therein;
Never can she speak, nor sing,
Nor smile but she shames herself.
Her silence wounds the fools,
Her discourse barely brushes them;
In one-liners she must chat,
Or speak with ambiguity.
Like some eccentric creature
At once they all examine her;
At once, a puritan stance
Throws her an insolent glance.
One priggish man, who rules his roost,
Encumbers her with grueling rules
And casts her back to needlework,
Despite her years[68] of pleasing toil.
One hellcat aggravates her,
And offers, in tolerant tones,
Out loud, some ambiguous praise,
Whispered, an affront sharply honed.
One hack writer shows up at her home,
Despite her orders crystal-clear,
And henceforth recaps far and near:

*I dropped by Mrs. So-and-so's;*
*There we have (Between you and me)*
*Talked about her brand new piece,*
*And my instruction sure won't hurt[69].*
One poet attacks her prose,
One prosodist attacks her verse;
They project on her a hundred quirks,
They publish then what they project;
About her they lie, they laugh, tell tales,
To the duped eyes of the universe.
Add to these sundry agonies
The kindnesses of all this stuff;
The songs, epigram, pamphlet,
Programmes regarding good apostles,
And you comprehend well what it's like
To be a bit less obtuse than the rest.
Good god! Vocation sad!
Yep, I renounce it for life;
Away, ink, pens, paper,
And verse's love, rage or folly!
Yet no; hasten back with your glare,
Confront all this clamorous strife!
Ah! you know how I may be saved
From all the ills you deal me.

–Translated by Olchar E. Lindsann

from *Les Annales Romantiques, ed. Charles Malo.* 1829. Janet: Paris, p. 243 (from the collection of the Revenant Archive); and *Oeuvres complètes de Madame la princesse Constance de Salm*, Vol. 2. Firmin-Didot / Arthus Bertrand: Paris, pp. 245-48.

---

**68** *Après quinze ans*, or "after fifteen years". I've been unable to scan "fifteen" without sacrificing other key aspects of the line's content.

---

69 Conjectural *nuiront*. The original printing appears to contain a typo (*nwront*).

*Projet d'uniforme*

Les citoyennes de la république, demandent à s'organiser en corps mobile volontaire et à s'habiller
aux frais de leurs maris. Elles promettent de garder la discipline toujours et le silence ......quelquefois.

*Gustave Mornes, **Projected Uniform**. c.1848. Aubert: Paris. Revenant Archive.*

*This cartoon mocks the upsurge of feminist activism in the wake of the 1848 Revolution, via the "absurd" notion of*
*women in the military:* "The Republic's female citizens, demanding to be organised into a mobile volun-
teer corps and to be dressed anew by their husbands. They promise to keep discipline always and
silence . . . occasionally."          *Yo-ho-ho, eh?*

135

# New from mOnocle-Lash

***Soul-roulette: Transmutations of Nerval,*** *by Gérard de Nerval and Retorico Unentesi.* Experimental and 'pataphysical transductions of poetry by the early avant-gardist Gérard de Nerval, rendered by the mysterious Retorico Unentesi of the Institute for Study & Application, Kohoutenberg. Padded out with extensive front-matter by eminent dead persons and an epic appendix elaborating & tangentiating upon the seams & merging of translation & poetic creation.

***Sound Rituals,*** *by Jim Leftwich & billy bob beamer.* "...an evocative apparatus that generates images in the ear and auditory revelations for the eyes. In a frequently disjointed consciousness reflective of the the exploding hybrids we all live a grand sweeping music arrives that compels us to reorient outside the delusion of self and adapt to worlds superimposed, alternatively transparent and opaque, full of sudden illumination and flittering shards fading into some nameless space only this poetry can describe. At a time when even the concept of truth seems forever elusive in this liturgy we are offered the opportunity to discover firsthand and immediately what pure unfiltered experience reveals." – Jake Berry.
*Forward by John M. Bennett*

## In Preparation for the mOnocle-Lash Revenants Series

The Revenant Series imprint publishes translations, histories, and new editions of works related to the 19th Century avant-garde, including the Romanticist, Frenetic, Occultist, Utopian Socialist, Bohemian, Parnassian, Anarchist, Decadent, and Symbolist communities.

Coming August 2018: ***Cinders from 'Fire and Flame',*** *by Philothée O'Neddy.* New translations from the signature 1833 collection of the Bouzingo co-founder, one of the most influential, yet forgotten, writers of the Romanticist avant-garde. An appetizer for a forthcoming full-length anthology.

***Long-Term Anthologies in Preparation:*** Estimated 2019-20 Release: *The Frenetic Feminine* (Anthology of Female founders of the avant-garde, c.1820–40), *Incoherent Footprints of the Rabid Black Cat* (Anthology of the Hydropathes, Incoherents, and Chat Noir groups c.1880–1900) & an anthology focusing on the role of dancing in the Romanticist Avant-Garde, c.1830–50. Estimated 2020 Release: *Tales of the Bouzingo* (Anthology of the first self-declared Avant-Garde collective, 1829–34).

***Eventual Projects under Consideration:*** Who knows what order or schedule? Vocal enthusiasm or Volunteers can affect it: Forgotten Avant-Gardists from the *Annales Romantiques* / *The Occult Avant-Garde 1830–1850* / Alphonse Karr, *Stingers from Les Gûepes* / Thomas Hood, *Poems on Poverty* / *The Battle of 'Hernani'* / *Gautier, Politics, & the Cult of Art* / etc. etc.

July, A.Da. 102  /  A.H. 188  /  2018 C.E.

**mOnocle-Lash Anti-Press**
## REVENANT SERIES
monoclelash.wordpress.com
monoclelash@gmail.com

# Rêvenance

## A Zine of Hauntings from Underground Histories

Issue No. 5        October 2018 (A.Da. 102, A.H. 188)

**Special Feature: Pipelets Under Attack!**

## Featuring

**The Dead**: : Philothée O'Neddy / Thomas Hood / Marceline Debord-Valmore / John Everett Millais / Sapeck / Célestin Nanteuil / J.-C. Sailer / The Mapah Ganneau / Eugène Sue / Cham / Faustin Betbedder / Gustave Karr / Harriet Preston / Arthur Verneuil / J. Grand-Carteret / & Others

**& The Living**: Olchar E. Lindsann / Elizabeth Birdsall

*Rêvenance* is dedicated to the forgotten or untold histories of 19th Century avant-garde and dissenting countercultures. It promotes historiography practiced as game, as activism, as transgenerational collaboration, as communal memory, which running athwart the academic, refuses to describe history as finished, and does not stand apart to observe its object from a distance, in the posture of false 'objectivity' which Power always assumes. Instead: a *committed* historiography, which does not stand outside the stream of time or apart from its object: intellectual and precise, yet ludic and multi-form, one moment manifest as an essay, the next as a poem. A historiography created *within* the utopian fringe, and for the same community, responsive to our changing conditions, needs, and desires. A historiography that *we take personally*, merging imperceptibly into experiments in daily life, social praxis, and thought.

The journal is closely integrated with the Revenant Archive of roughly 600 books, prints, manuscripts, and personal items from the 19th Century avant-garde, and much of the material is drawn from the archive's material. The journal explores forgotten and newly-discovered histories of avant-garde, radical activist, utopian, and other underground countercultures. While the primary focus is on the 19th Century, earlier and later material is also welcome, and contributions directly connecting counter-cultural movements and strategies across time are particularly encouraged. The primary goal is to explore histories, communities, and themes that are not consistently represented elsewhere. *Rêvenance* seeks to develop a community of independent DIY researchers who see historical work as part of a communal praxis directed toward contemporary and future change; it is a laboratory in which countercultural history is transmuted, reflected and disseminated in the current lifestyle, writing, music, art, and thought of present-day communities of dissent or otherness.

**Edited by Olchar E. Lindsann**
*Rights retained by translators & living writers*
All other texts in the public domain
Lindsann's translations: Creative
Commons, Non-Commercial Share-Alike;
please inform us of republications

Oct., A.Da. 102
A.H. 188
2018 A.D.

mOnocle-Lash Anti-Press
Revenants Series
monoclelash.wordpress.com
revenant-archive.blogspot.com
monoclelash@gmail.com
bouzingo.blogspot.com

Post: c/o Olchar Lindsann, Editor / 2027 Mountain View Terrace SW /
Roanoke, VA 24015 / USA (**U**nfortunate, **S**ad **A**nathema)

# CONTENTS

*All uncredited translations are by Olchar E. Lindsann.*

*Many of the source texts are available online at* gallica.bnf.fr *and/or at* archive.org.

*Betbader 'Pipelet' cartoons © Victoria and Albert Museum, London.*

***Cover image by Olchar E. Lindsann***, collaged from: Célestin Nanteuil, *Profundities of Love* and *Publuc Baths* (c.1840-50), A.B., *Prado* (Undated, c.1835-40), Merwart, *Editorial Breakfast at the Chat Noir* (1887), Anonymous frontispiece to J. Bouchardy's *Paris the Bohemian* (1842), & Cham, *Social Studies: The New God* (c.1848). All constituent images photocopied from originals held in the Revenant Archive (neither digitised nor sliced up).

**Send Submissions & Correspondence to monoclelash@gmail.com**

# Forward

The predominant thread that emerged while assembling this issue of *Rêvenance* is economic. The issue starts out looking at poverty by way of its frequent remedy, Crime, through the lens of french Frenetic Romanticism in a pair of pieces by two co-founders of the Bouzingo group (c.1829-33) – an artist and a poet – presenting highwaymen as agents of social rebellion. Next, a pair of English offerings – again an artist and a poet – from the following generation examine the links between poverty, prostitution, suicide, and bourgeois society's moral hypocrisy. The centrist cartoonist Cham ridicules autodidact workers in an 1848 anarchist book-shop, then the self-taught labourer J.-C. Sailer writes of the socialist movement of 1841 in terms reminiscent of the Frenetic Romantics, from a workers' anthology compiled by Olinde Rodrigues, coiner of the term 'avant-garde'. The latter, as it happens, had been an early theorist of the proto-socialist Saint-Simonian movement, which in turn appears in this issue in the form of a right-wing satire. The movement also had a major influence on the socialist-feminist-occult Evadamist movement of 'The Mapah' Ganneau, represented here by one of his more sober pamphlets demanding universal suffrage for the male and female working class. Marceline Debordes-Valmore condemns the violent suppression of workers' anti-monarchist demonstrations.

This economic theme is continued through this issue's special feature (are these becoming a trend?) on the multi-general feud between "Pipelets" or Concierges and the writers and artists of Paris. The revenant we have uncovered proves as multi-faceted as that in last issue's feature. We find a unionisation movement among a massive sector of the service industry which has since disappeared, and accompanied the economic and infrastructure shift from rural to urban tenancy. We also find unexpected interweavings with Bohemian subculture: the Socialist-Romanticist novelist Eugène Sue created the nickname and popular stereotype of the "Pipelet" in 1842, and forty years later the avant-satirists Sapeck and Jouy of the Hydropaths / Chat Noir groups targeted them in a gleefully spiteful magazine dedicated to their ridicule. As too often happens, what for the Bohemians was a public gag in the spirit of Fluxus or Neoism was experienced by the targeted workers as a real attack that damaged their struggle for social respect.

I encourage, and would readily print, responses to the material presented, particularly in connection to contemporary conditions (the current complicity of what is left of Bohemia with gentrification creates plenty of analogous encounters . . . ). The same is true of last issue's feature on the Badouillards, and indeed anything presented in *Rêvenance*.

The issue closes with a late-comer to *last* issue's feature on early Parisian dance-club culture: an article on police raids on licentious dances from Karr's self-published mag *The Wasps*.

# The Cavern (1855)

*by Célestin Nanteuil*

*Célestin Nanteuil [pronounce: Say-less-tan Nan-tuey-eh] was a co-founder of the* **Bouzingo** *[Booze-on-joe] group, which spearheaded the micro-community known as Frenetic Romanticism, a fusion of extremist Romanticism with popular Gothic subculture. This print depicts a familiar scene from the gothic novels so dear to Nanteuil and other Frenetic Romantics: a company of armed bandits divide the spoil of a recent crime. Unlike most depictions, Nanteuil places the 'exciting' bandits in the background; while in the foreground, the print focuses on their families cooking dinner and playing. The bandits are ironically de-'romanticiszed' and revealed as simply impoverished, desperate family-men, practicing a trade beyond the bounds of bourgeois Labour. This picture is from an 1855 issue of the* **Illustrated London News***; it was probably lifted from a French newspaper and may have illustrated a particular story.* <u>Revenant Archive.</u>

~^~^~^~^~^~^~^~^~^~^~^~^~^~^~^~^~^~^~^~^~^~^~^~^~^~^~^~^~^~

*This poem by the ultra-Romanticist Philothée O'Neddy [pronounce: Feel-o-tay O'Neddy] is a wicked example of the dark, avant-gothic sub-current known as* **Frenetic Romanticism**, *of which O'Neddy was a leading practitioner and which established the literary language built upon in the following generations by Baudelaire, Lautréamont, Genonceaux, and Bataille – in particular, one recognises in O'Neddy's character of Itobal one of the models for Maldoror. He is also a likely influence on J.-C. Sailer's poem elsewhere in this issue. O'Neddy was a co-founder of the* **Jeunes-France** *[say: June-Frahnce] /* **Bouzingo** *[Boose-on-joe] collective and a key early theorist of the avant-garde, which he referred to as "the Outlaws of Thought" – an interesting comment in connection with this text, especially in conjunction with the preceding etching of highwaymen by his comrade and fellow Jeunes-France member Nanteuil. Escousse, cited in the epigraph, was another young frenetic poet who had recently committed suicide following the failure of his play in the face of a Classicist critical campaign against it; not every "Battle" ended like* **Hernani**.

## Ninth Night:

# Incantation (1833)

*by Philothée O'Neddy*

My hardships and my blood determine my career;
My blood speaks to me, to me, 'tis my blood that I hear:
I do not think, me, I have sensations,
And my simple desires merit my passions!

Victor Escousse.

To his palace abhorred beneath boulders deep-bored,

Itobal comes alone; underneath the low lintel,

He snatches up his gun and his bronze-tinted sword;

Then, on a bed of rushes, branch dead and brittle,

His spent height allows to tumble soil-ward.

But in vain this throatslicer,[1] whom fatigue so exceeds,

Ceasing three days of marching and bloodspattered fight,

Seeks slumber here within his cavern's frigid bite:

Profound vertigo on his obsession feeds.

---

1 *égorgeur*. A neologism when O'Neddy used it, the word has only rarely appeared since then, hence I've chosen a less familiar phrase than the common English "cutthroat"

– A thousand curses! quoth he behind his bite:

There, close upon my ear, a swarm musters and roils;

My spasming muscles convulse, my lifeblood boils;

You would think I was on rageous anthracite!

I know not which cruel sprite is so spitefully frantic

To thus strip an old wolf of the slumber he's won:

So what? Do I not own an arcane magic,

To souse my senses with a balm lethargic,

For three entire reigns of night and of the sun? . . .

– Hey there! Do you stir, dull and vacant skulls

Of all the craven viles[2] whom my knife-hand has splayed!

Skulls, who slumber longside broad well-trampled ways,

In the water of wells, in the forests baleful,

Bring it on! Bring it on! Upon the winds take wing.

Profit then from the dark, in your advent aerial;

Then, alongside faint screams, with wheezings funereal,

Around my bedside valence dance, dance madly circling![3]

He'd scarcely dared to issue these demonic bulls,

Than, through the cloven rocks, boistrously in there bound,

Upon amber rays, a cortege of skulls,

By whom swiftly the bloodspattered bedside is crowned.

The dance tightens round, tis convulsed and whirled amiss;

And beguiled, mesmerised by the arhythmic course

Of psalms that the ball is buzzing in its bliss,

Fervently our highwayman to slumber deep is forced.

Yo! all you moralists, what's that about remorse?

*trans. Olchar E. Lindsann*

*from* **Feu et flamme**, ed. Marcel Hervier. 1926. Bibliothèque Romantique: Paris. <u>Revenant Archive.</u>

---

2 O'Neddy is employing an adjective, *vils,* as a noun. His love for such grammatical disruptions and transpositions kept his verse nearly unpublishable even in Romanticist publications.

3 *en rond*, i.e., in a ring. In frenetic Romanticist circles, this was understood to refer to the dionysian *rond de sabbat*, or witches' dance – which in turn was related to the Infernal Gallop, the favourite dance of the frenetics. This was essentially the same as contemporary punk circle-pits, and in which dancers who tripped were routinely trampled (see *Révenance 4* for a lithograph portraying the dance.)

~^~^~^~^~^~^~^~^~^~^~^~^~^~^~^~^~^~^~^~^~^~^~^~^~^~^~^~^~^~

# The Bridge of Sighs (1858)
## by John Everett Millais

*The painter John Everett Millais was a co-founder of the Pre-Raphaelite Brotherhood, which collectively pioneered the visual idioms of the British Symbolist movement. At the time that he drew this response to Thomas Hood's poem on the facing page, Millais had begun to abandon the formally challenging, spatially flattening language of his earlier work for a more main-stream illusionism for which a commercial market existed.*

~^~^~^~^~^~^~^~^~^~^~^~^~^~^~^~^~^~^~^~^~^~^~^~^~^~

*The English poet Thomas Hood was best known as a writer of comic verse, but his work often cham-pioned progressive social causes and satirized the hypocrisies of capitalist society (cf. his little epigram on the commercialization of art in* **Rêvenance 3***). There is no trace of humour (though some poi-sonous irony) in this both gentle and remarkably bitter poem on a homeless women driven first to prostitution, then to suicide. It was quite popular in the decades after its publication, inspired several graphic interpretations including that by Millais on the facing page, and was cited by the famous-ly-harsh Edgar Poe as a near-perfect text.*

# The Bridge of Sighs (1844)

### by Thomas Hood

One more Unfortunate,
Weary of breath,
Rashly importunate,
Gone to her death!

Take her up tenderly,
Lift her with care;
Fashion'd so slenderly
Young, and so fair!

Look at her garments
Clinging like cerements;
Whilst the wave constantly
Drips from her clothing;
Take her up instantly,
Loving, not loathing.

Touch her not scornfully;
Think of her mournfully,
Gently and humanly;
Not of the stains of her,
All that remains of her
Now is pure womanly.

Make no deep scrutiny
Into her mutiny
Rash and undutiful:
Past all dishonour,
Death has left on her
Only the beautiful.

Still, for all slips of hers,
One of Eve's family—
Wipe those poor lips of hers
Oozing so clammily.

Loop up her tresses
Escaped from the comb,
Her fair auburn tresses;
Whilst wonderment guesses
Where was her home?

Who was her father?
Who was her mother?
Had she a sister?
Had she a brother?
Or was there a dearer one
Still, and a nearer one
Yet, than all other?

Alas! for the rarity
Of Christian charity
Under the sun!
O, it was pitiful!
Near a whole city full,
Home she had none.

Sisterly, brotherly,
Fatherly, motherly
Feelings had changed:
Love, by harsh evidence,
Thrown from its eminence;
Even God's providence
Seeming estranged.

Where the lamps quiver
So far in the river,
With many a light
From window and casement,
From garret to basement,
She stood, with amazement,
Houseless by night.

The bleak wind of March
Made her tremble and shiver;
But not the dark arch,
Or the black flowing river:
Mad from life's history,
Glad to death's mystery,
Swift to be hurl'd —
Anywhere, anywhere
Out of the world!

In she plunged boldly —
No matter how coldly
The rough river ran —
Over the brink of it,
Picture it — think of it,

Dissolute Man!
Lave in it, drink of it,
Then, if you can!

Take her up tenderly,
Lift her with care;
Fashion'd so slenderly,
Young, and so fair!

Ere her limbs frigidly
Stiffen too rigidly,
Decently, kindly,
Smooth and compose them;
And her eyes, close them,
Staring so blindly!

Dreadfully staring
Thro' muddy impurity,
As when with the daring
Last look of despairing
Fix'd on futurity.

Perishing gloomily,
Spurr'd by contumely,
Cold inhumanity,
Burning insanity,
Into her rest. —
Cross her hands humbly
As if praying dumbly,
Over her breast!

Owning her weakness,
Her evil behaviour,
And leaving, with meekness,
Her sins to her Saviour!

from Thomas Hood, ***The Poetical Works of Thomas Hood***. 1873. *James Miller, Publisher, New York.*

Cham, **Social Studies**. 1848. Lithograph. Bureau de Charivari: Paris. *This must be one of the earliest depictions of an Anarchist Bookshop—produced within months of the 1848 Revolution, before which such literature was quite dangerous to circulate, and only eight years after Pierre-Joseph Proudhon, named the movement. The simple stand's signage reads: PROUDHON REPARE [sic] OF ALL KINDS RESTORED THE OLD TO NEW. The proprietor is clearly a cobbler by trade, and, we are meant to infer, semi-literate—an insult to Anarchism's working-class, often self-taught adherents. The customer is an 18th century aristocrat to parody of the movement's intellectual supporters. The caption reads: "Reassembly, repair and re-soling of old political, financial and social systems"*
<u>from the Collection of the Revenant Archive.</u>

~^~^~^~^~^~^~^~^~^~^~^~^~^~^~^~^~^~^~^~^~^~^~^~^~^~^~^~^~^~

*This poem was written by the typesetter J.-C. Sailer [Say-lay], and published in an anthology of* **Workers' Socialist Poems** *edited by Olinde Rodrigues, the Saint-Simonist theorist-activist (see p. 19) who had first coined and defined the term "avant-garde" in its cultural sense 16 years earlier. Sailer was probably self-taught, as ridiculed on the previous page by the centrist cartoonist Cham. He had a collection of poems (possibly either an ephemeral pamphlet/proto-zine or unpublished but circulating fair-copied manuscript/s), but I can find no further trace of it or him. The misanthropic first section of the piece, the protestations of camaraderie, and the weird imagery reveal the strong influence of Frenetic Romanticism, particularly Philothée O'Neddy, whose poem opens this issue and who owned a copy of this anthology, and may have known Rodrigues (probably not Sailer) personally.*

# To My Friend (1841)

*by J.-C. Sailer*

## I

My exposure to humans, which curdled my spirit,
Turned me into a skeptic, callously to jeer it:
Such the stone, that the iron's shock provokes, ignites,
Grinds down, hones it, to craft a broadsword that can smite.

Snickering, slandering, I stropped the epigram
Against all belief, and, soldier of accident,
I loved to fire my barbs upon the filaments
That twist encircling a heart with hollow shams.

I suffered so, my friend! Belief, and poetry,
Aspiration, love, all deserted my days;
My being was interred entirely in hate.

Thus our end seemed to me a vast perplexity;
I thought myself enclasped by this fatal quandary:
Either happiness or fame – obscurity or misery!

# II

Your heart partook and pacified that agony
Which took life but refused to hand me to the grave.
You restored to me hope, fellowship, and my faith,
And the tunes of my lute to ardent ecstasies.

Be ye blessed! Because fortune invests your life
With your tenderest gifts, with your dearest treasures;
Your share must be immense of honours and pleasures;
Know a thousand delights without even one sole strife.

With such euphoria my gaze contemplates thee,
Apostle of progress, who by example leads
Labour, the union, loyalty, and peace!

Be ye blessed! We attain such adventurous feats . . .
I trust the days to come, and await the messiah
My hands within your hands, our eyes up in the skies!

–*trans. Olchar E. Lindsann*

from *Poésies sociales des ouvriers*, ed. Olinde Rodrigues. 1841. Paulin: Paris. *From the Revenant Archive.*

*The tiny occultist-feminist-socialist movement known as* **Evadamism***, (Eve-Adam-ism) despite its extreme obscurity, had a major influence on occultism and hermeticism in the late 19th Century, particularly through Eliphas Levi, one its most active proponents. This fascinating and intensely strange little group, led by the Romanticist sculptor-turned spiritualist Messiah known as the Mapah Ganneau [Gahn-noh]. Revenant Editions has already published a mystical-feminist Evadamist manifesto as a separate pamphlet (***Baptism-Marriage***); here is a more mythopoeic political statement advocating that the Peoples (the masses, the lower classes) of the world unite together (foreshadowing of Marx's international proletariat and the Wobblies' 'One Big Union') – under the leadership of the French People, cast in the role of Christ sacrificed upon the cross of Waterloo, in a mythification of society not unlike that of Blake (with whom it is unlikely he was familiar, however).*

# Evadamist Manifesto for Electoral Reform (1840)

*by the Mapah Simon Ganneau*

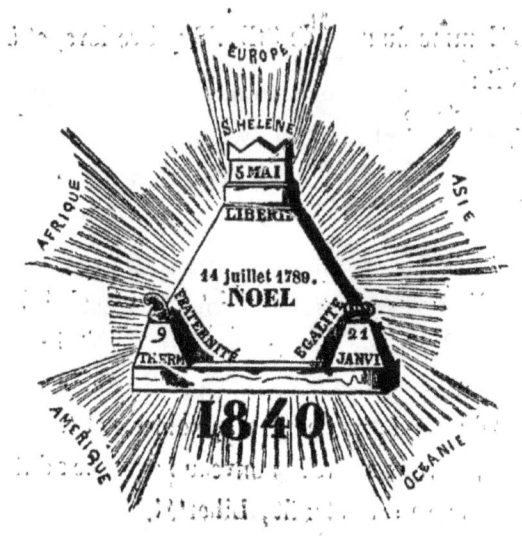

*I am no longer going to say to the People:*
*Render unto Caesar that which is Caesar's!*
*Caesar's mission is at an end.*
*But I am going to say unto Caesar:*
*Render to God that which is God's!*
*Who is God?*
*God is the People.*

And the Word was made Man in a man named of Jesus;

And the Word was made People in a people named France;

And the Word unity Man was made flesh in the breast of a Virgin named Mary;

And the Word unity People was made flesh in the breast of a Virgin named LIBERTY.

What is the Word?

The Word is LOVE.

And the Mother of the Christ Man gave birth in a stable;

And the Mother of the Christ People gave birth in a bastille.

I tell you truly: the Holy Virgin Mary of the Heavens, the Holy Virgin Liberty of the earth, are the GRAND-MOTHER, THE GRAND PARIAH, THE GENESIAC EVE.

In 1789, lived a Man by the name of Sieyes[4] who rose up, and in the face of the Nobility and the Clergy said:

What is the Third Estate?

Nothing.

What should it be?

Everything.

To these simple words, the violent voice of Mirabeau responded: The great are only great because we are at their knees; raise us up, and we shall be greater than they.

As soon as the Tennis Court Oath burst forth, Nobility and Clergy were overturned, and from the chaos of the Estates-General issued the new Logos, the holy doctrine Sovereignty People: and an immense cry resounded, Liberty!

From this sacred name, the dawn of the great day was created, the gods of despotism were crushed, the Bastille, their monstrous symbol, toppled; and from the old world's wreckage was erected, resplendent in glory and love, LIBERTY OUR HOLY MOTHER, with lacerated sides from which emerged, on the 14 July 89,[5] THE FRENCH PEOPLE, THE MESSIAH OF PEOPLES.

Such is the origin, the seed of this french revolution which transfigured the world; successively called National Assembly, Constituent, Legislative, Convention, Directory, Consulate, Empire, Restoration, July Revolution, at the current moment it is named:

ELECTORAL REFORM! . . .

What is Electoral Reform?

Electoral Reform is the matrix of the French Revolution's resplendent fruit.

The resplendent fruit, it is the holy doctrine Sovereignty, become People.

It consists of propositions so self-evident, that once posed they are resolved; it consists of such gravity, that once attacked they strike instantly to death, if they do not regenerate.

Let the deaf hear, let the blind see! for, in politics as in physics, expansion is due to compression.

Sons of Liberty, listen!

ELECTORAL REFORM, on today 14 July 1840, is formulated thus:

In 1789 what was the Third Estate? (The bourgeoisie.)

Nothing.

From 1789 to 1840, what has the Third Estate become? (The bourgeoisie._

4 Revolutionary leader Emmanuel Sieyes published his pamphlet *What is the Third Estate?* in 1789.
5 The date of the storming of the Bastille.

Everything.

In 1840 what is the People?

Nothing.

What shall it be?

Everything! . . .

May this formula be consecrated! and that it may be consecrated, Daughters and Sons of the world's martyrs, unite among yourselves! Let your spirits be elevated to the great spirit of your Fathers; let their magnum opus, the Revolution, that terrible and sacred childbirth of United Humanity,  rise up before you in all its majesty, and the overjoyed heart of dignity and joy, charming children of Giants of the Federation, shout along with us, in sacred ecstasy: PEACE! PEACE! PEACE!

I tell you truly:

On today 14 July 1840, fiftieth anniversary of the revolution is the day of the French People's Peace, of the CHRIST-PEOPLE dead for the Peoples' salvation.

Peoples our brothers, are you listening? he cries to you from his cradle:  Liberty, Equality, Fraternity!

Peoples our brothers, are you listening? he cries to you from the height of his cross of Waterloo:  Liberty, Equality, Fraternity!

Peoples our brothers, are you listening? he cries to you from his tomb:  Liberty, Equality, Fraternity?

Peoples our brothers, have great faith and good hope; for the hour of the resurrection, of the grand Passover and the grand Federation is at hand.

Peoples our brothers, in the name of the Mother of all love, of the great Eve, of sacred Liberty, recall that the point where Caesar ends is where Man begins; that the point where Man begins is the Brother . . . Fraternity! . . .

MY SISTERS AND MY BROTHERS.

Factionalism is Division, Misery and Night.

Association[6] is Unity, Joy and Light.

Hear this parable and let it be for you a spark of Life and Regeneration.

---

6 The early 19th Century term used broadly for what in mid-century would become known as Socialism, and more narrowly as as what would become unionisation.

The grains of sand were complaining to God, saying:

The slightest wind stirs us up and drives us from coast to coast upon the rocks which rip us apart; the slightest drop of water engulfs us; we are the plaything of the elements and the pasture[7] of the smallest pebble and the beach which devours us; and in their anguish all cried out to God for mercy.

God responds to them ASSOCIATION.

Sisters and brothers in wretchedness, associate with us and we shall become the giants, the new armature of humanity transfigured, which is to say associated, united! . . .

The law of Association is known in the atomic world as Attraction,[8] in the intellectual world as Love.

I tell you truly: the matrix of Attraction, of Love and its magnificent fruit Expansion, is the Evadian Unity.[9]

Evadian Unity is the Epic Poem of human life in all of these modes of manifestation, and the State of Liberty, Equality, Fraternity, Expansion, Love, Harmony, Unity and Sovereignty.

Within Evadian Unity all are called, all are selected, all are rehabilitated.


From our pallet[10] in our city of Paris, the great Eda[11] of the earth, today, 14 July 1840, Day of Peace for the People of France, and of the Peoples' Messiah.

In the name of the great Evadah, in the name of the Great God, Mother, Father.

From Paris, to the Universe.

EXPANSION, LOVE.

**The Mapah.**

*"There was only dust and nothingness, a tear of Love dripped from the Mother's breast turned it into Life and Light."*

– trans. Olchar E. Lindsann

from Le Mapah [Simon Ganneau], Untitled Pamphlet [Opuscule sur la reforme électuale et le droit d'association]. July 14, 1840. Self-Published (printed by Malteste): Paris.

---

7 Also used figuratively as "lifeblood", an undertone with which Ganneau is playing.

8 *Attraction* is a key term in the system of Fourier, one of the main inspirations for Evadamist theory. *Unity,* in the next sentence, is another.

9 *Evadienne*. Ganneau uses the feminine version of his movement's neologistic name (*Evadamiste* being the masculine form). I have rendered the *-ienne* ending as *-ian* in accordance with the common translation of Saint-Simon's female (and sometimes all) followers as *Saint-Simonians*.

10 *grabat*. A makeshift bed; the modern equivalent might be a futon.

11 *Éda*. I can find no trace of this word or proper noun. It may possibly be a further truncation of the portmanteau word "Évadah" (the Evadian/Edadamist hermaphroditic deity).

*Marceline Debordes-Valmore [Day-bored Val-more] was one of the most influential female avant-gardists of the 1830s (see* **Rêvenance** *#2). This outraged poem reacts to the massacre by Monarchist forces of revolting silk-industry workers in Lyon. 2-600 were killed, 10,000 deported or imprisoned.*

# LYONS, 1834

### *by Marceline Debordes-Valmore*

We cannot even bury these dead of ours ;
Too great the cost of priestly funerals:
So they lie stark, all torn with cruel balls,
Awaiting coffins, crosses, and remorse !

Now is the assassin king ! He stalks to fetch
The price of blood from out the treasury ;
He slays, in passing, some defenceless wretch,
Yet still insatiate with blood is he.

God sees him. God will gather like bruised flowers
The souls of babes and women who to him
Are fled, — the air with outraged souls 1 is dim,
On earth men wade in blood, — Merciful Powers !

The spirit haunts its desecrated corpse :
But all too dear are priestly funerals ;
So our dead lie all torn with cruel balls,
Awaiting coffins, crosses, and remorse.

Wear black, my sisters ! — Weep as ne'er before ;
They will not let us take our slain away ;
They make one heap of their dishonored clay ;
And, God, thou knowest that never arms they bore !

trans.  Harriet W. Preston

from *The Memoirs of Madame Debordes-Valmore,* trans. Harriet W. Preston. 1873. Roberts Brothers: Boston.

~^~^~^~^~^~^~^~^~^~^~^~^~^~^~^~^~^~^~^~^~^~^~^~^~

*Saint-Simonianism was the most prominent socialist movement in France from the 1820s into the 1840s, and its influence permeated the network of Parisian countercultures. After the death of its founder, Clude-Henri Rouvroy, comte de Saint-Simon, it evolved as a utopian, technocratic, feminist-inspired movement couched in religious terms and led by the charismatic 'Father Enfantin' after a power-struggle between him and Olinde Rodrigues (see introduction on p.12). Their soup kitchens and free schools in working-class areas, combined with huge lectures and rallies attended by all classes, made them a real danger to the new capitalist "Liberal Monarchy" in the 1830s, and the community was destroyed by a public smear campaign and a series of show trials. In Hugo's **Les Misérables**, Combeferre is specifically mentioned as a reader of Saint-Simon's work, and Saint-Simonist ideas would, directly or indirectly, have infused the thought of the "Amis", as of the Jeunes-France / Bouzingo group (cf. O'Neddy and Nanteuil in this issue) on whom they were largely based.*

## The Saint-Simonians (1832)

Here is what the Saint-Simonians dreamed of.

Because while others riot for the republic and for Henri V, while the bousingots bait the people by presenting them with the lure of the guillotine, confiscations, mass levies and bankruptcy; while the carlists buy votes with pieces of false silver stamped with the monarch who just finished teething, the Saint-Simonians dream.[12]

What do the Saint-Simonians dream?

They dreamed of constructing railroads. It happened that industrialists had had the same idea a little earlier, and went more quickly than them, because one makes more railroads with iron and coal than with systems and words. Then the Saint-Simonians say: they're following our ideas.[13]

The day approaches when the Saint-Simonians will dream of giving leaves to trees and wool to sheep. We're assured that we owe to them the invention of slate roofs and roast lamb. When their works are extended further, they'll imagine that the course of rivers follows the slope of the

---

12 *Editor's Note:* Republicans advocated a moderate, liberal democracy; Henry V, grandson of the overthrown Charles X, was hailed by ultra-monarchists as the legitimate king; bousingots were ultra-Romanticist insurrectionary socialists; Carlists wanted an heir of the overthrown Bourbon dynasty on the Spanish throne. All held frequent and often violent street demonstrations. The *Figaro* was at this time owned by the only party not mentioned: the July Monarchy which had been in control since the 1830 Revolution, and bought the one-time opposition paper to attack the regime's enemies.

13 *Editor's Note:* Many leading Saint-Simonians were successful bankers, financiers, and industrialists, and later had great influence on the french rail system and the construction of the Suez Canal.

land. They lack nothing but to discover the free woman[14] to discover the moon, the sun, the stars, and M. de La Palisse's commentaries on death. For now, they've invented a system of general peace.

And here is their reasoning.

Everything has a beginning, a middle and an end; good or evil.

It's a question of evil.

The evil of the moment is disorder, it's dissidence of opinions, it's only the small beginnings of chaos. But, if we push chaos to its highest degree, to its apogee, it necessarily approaches its end.

Thus, there's nothing so close to peace as war; the more violent the war, the more it approaches peace. People who seek peace ought thus to strive towards war, those who want calm towards riot; those who want prosperity towards gossip of bankruptcy, those who want unity towards civil war.

That's what the Saint-Simonians thought, or at least, it's the necessary background of their findings. We'll continue.

Thus, the best means to have peace being to breathe on the flames of war, it's necessary to force the parties to come to blows; it's necessary to stir them up, to give them chiefs. One must search for the chiefs most opposed to [one's] interests that one can find, and in the greatest possible number. For the moment, only three present themselves: Henri V, the duke of Orleans, Napoleon II.

It's already nice enough.

You see from here the kingdom pulled in three different directions, which is the shortest road to unity, because by the strength of all this pulling, it will be torn; the more it's torn, the more pressing it will be to patch things up, the more quickly everyone will take care of reorganizing it.

It's annoying that only three kings of France present themselves, because by this method there will only be three parts to fight amongst themselves and destroy each other.

Other pretenders are begged to join up at the *Globe* offices, since the new government is

---

14 "The free woman": *La Femme Libre* (The Free Woman) was a Saint-Simonist journal founded in 1832, produced and published by women, and the first French feminist journal. The first issue of *La Femme Libre* came out in August 1832, several months after this March issue, but "free woman" was already being used as a slang/rhetorical term, from which the feminist journal probably took up the name. *Rêvenance* #3 contains a brief review of a book on the journal. A further joke here: hypocritically, the Saint-Simonist men found none of the actual female members worthy of fulfilling the female half of the dual papacy, leaving Enfantin in sole control; a group of men later sought her in Egypt.

Saint-Simonian clothing laced in the back, to demonstrate the mutual dependence of individuals within a community.

under the influence and inspiration of the doctrine, as the *Globe* is announcing.[15]

Temporarily, since there are only three, one must content oneself with this small amount of disorder and anarchy. Fine, fine, long live peace, burn houses, bring in foreigners. Long live peace! Fight, kill; long live peace. There's no peace possible as long as there's any house standing, as long as there's any law in effect. We've proved it, peace is born from disorder.

See how disorder will grow. Each of the three dukes could have three sons; on their deaths you will have nine kings of France, after these nine twenty-seven, after these twenty-seven eighty-one; then one day everyone will be king of France.

Then the disorder will be complete. When disorder can't go any further, when it's hit the limit, then order must arrive; when all the world is killed, there must be peace.

Here is, in our present situation, what the Saint-Simonians dreamed best:

"Put on the throne Henri V, the duke of Orleans and Napoleon II." (*Globe*, March 21)[16]

Why not also the king of Holland, Leopold of Belgium, Sultan Mahmoud, and Méhémed-Ali [Muhammad Ali], the viceroy of Egypt? Or indeed there's another option, which is to give the crown to M. Enfantin who is *the greatest of giants of the earth.* (*Globe*, March 22)[17]

M. Enfantin, *who is surrounded by a halo of majesty.* (*Globe*.)

M. Enfantin, *in front of whom all heads bend respectfully.* (*Globe*.)

M. Enfantin, *who appears in the middle of these boys with his face radiant.* (*Globe*.)

Amen.

–trans. Elizabeth Birdsall

from *Figaro* Year 8, No. 33, March 23, 1832. from the collection of the Revenant Archive.

---

15 **Editor's Note:** Thanks to its technocratic basis, Saint-Simonianists were often seduced by the hope for an "Enlightened Tyrant" to establish their system and then hand power over to the benevolent technocratic bureaucracy. Later, many members of the movement supported the totalitarian regime of Napoleon III, son of Napoleon II named below, also the head of an Imperialist faction.

16 **Translator's Note:** The duke of Orleans is of course Louis-Philippe I, officially king at this point (and for the next several years, until the 1848 revolution.)

17 **Translator's Note:** The *Globe* was a Saint-Simonian journal run by the "charismatic" subgroup of Saint-Simonians after Saint-Simon's death. M. Enfantin was the leader of that subgroup.

~^~^~^~^~^~^~^~^~^~^~^~^~^~^~^~^~^~^~^~^~^~^~^~^~^~^~^~^~

# Special Feature: The Pipelets Under Attack!

This issue's special feature, like the last, rather took me by surprise: it began as a little peek at an avant-garde satirical sheet, and led to an exploration of domestic life, labour organising, and social stereotypes over half a decade. Its focus is are the tens of thousands of Parisian concierges, whose jobs combined those of Rental Manager, Porter, Mail Service, Security, and Property Manager, and who made the capitalist urban rental system function (to the extent that it did, or does). The popular image of these workers was established in 1842 as the *Pipelet* ("Peep-eh-lay").

~^~^~^~^~^~^~^~^~^~^~^~^~

*The novels and plays of the Romanticist Eugène Sue, infused with Socialist and anti-clerical propaganda, exerted a phenomenal mass appeal nearly as great as that of Victor Hugo. His work's combination of mawkish sentimentality, gothic-horror overtones, and social rage exerted a distinctive influence on frenetic Romanticism (his novel **Lautreamont** provided the author of **Maldoror** with his pseudonym). His character of Pipelet, a typical gossipy concierge of a working-class apartment building, came to epitomize that workforce throughout the century and lent them their nickname in slang.*

## from *The Mysteries of Paris* (1842-43)

*by Eugène Sue*

M. Pipelet entered the lodge with a grave, magisterial air. He was about sixty years of age, comfortably fat, with a large, broad countenance, strongly resembling in its cast and style the faces carved upon the far-famed nutcrackers of Nuremberg; a nose, of more than ordinary proportions, helping to complete the likeness. An old and dingy-looking hat, with a very deep brim, surmounted the whole. Alfred, who adhered to this upper ornament as tenaciously as his wife did to her Brutus wig, was further attired in an ancient green coat, with immense flaps turned up with grease,—if so might be described the bright and shiny patches of long-accumulated dirt, which had given an entirely different hue to some portions of the garment. But, though clad in a hat and coat esteemed by Pipelet and his wife as closely resembling full dress, Alfred had not laid aside the modest emblem of his trade, but from his waist uprose the buff-coloured triangular front of his leathern apron, partly concealing a waistcoat boasting nearly as great a variety of colours as did the patchwork counterpane of Madame Pipelet.

The porter's recognition of Rodolph as he entered was gracious in the extreme; but, alas! he smiled a melancholy welcome, and his countenance and languid air marked a man of secret sorrow.

"Alfred," said Madame Pipelet, when she had introduced her two companions, "here is a gentleman after the apartment on the fourth floor, and we have only been waiting for you to drink a glass of cordial he sent for."

This delicate attention won for Rodolph the entire trust and confidence of the melancholy porter, who, touching the brim of his hat, said, in a deep bass voice worthy of being employed in a cathedral:

"We shall give the gentleman every satisfaction as porters, and, doubtless, he will act the same by us as a lodger; 'birds of a feather flock together,' as the proverb says." Then, interrupting himself, M. Pipelet anxiously added, "Providing, sir, you are not a painter!"

"No, I am not a painter, but a plain merchant's clerk."

"My most humble duty to you, sir. I congratulate you that Nature did not make you one of those monsters called artists."

"Artists, monsters!" returned Rodolph. "Tell me, pray, why you style them so."

Instead of replying, M. Pipelet elevated his clasped hands towards the ceiling, and allowed a heavy sound, between a grunt and a groan, to escape his overcharged breast.

"You must know, sir," said Madame Pipelet, in a low tone, to Rodolph, "that painters have embittered Alfred's life; they have worried my poor old dear almost out of his senses, and made him half stupefied, as you see him now." Then speaking loud, she added, in a caressing tone, "Oh, never mind the blackguard, there's a dear, but try and forget all about it, or you will be ill, and unable to eat the nice tripe I have got for your dinner."

"Let us hope I shall have courage and firmness enough for all things," replied M. Pipelet, with a dignified and resigned air; "but he has done me much harm; he has been my persecutor, almost my executioner,—long have I suffered, but now I despise him! Ah," said he, turning to Rodolph, "never allow a painter to enter your doors; they are the plague—the ruin—the destruction of a house!"

"You have, then, had a painter lodging with you, I presume?"

"Unhappily, sir, I did have one," replied M. Pipelet, with much bitterness, "and that one named Cabrion. Ah!"

At the recollections brought back by this name, the porter's declaration of courage and endurance utterly failed him, and again his clenched fists were raised, as though to invoke the vengeance he had so lately described himself as despising.

"And was this individual the last occupant of the chamber I am about engaging?" inquired Rodolph.

"No, no! The last lodger was an excellent young man named M. Germain. No, this Cabrion had the room before he came. Ah, sir, since Cabrion left, he has all but driven me stark staring mad!"

*Madame Pipelet*. by Faustin Betbedder, 1870-71. *Napoleon III and Empress Eugénie are portrayed as Mr. and Mrs. Pipelet, in these two prints produced immediately after the regime's fall.*

"Did you, then, so much regret him?" asked Rodolph.

"Regret him! Regret Cabrion!" screamed the astounded porter; "why, only imagine, M. Bras Rouge paid him two quarters' rent to induce him to quit the place, for, unluckily, he had taken his apartments for a term. What a scamp he was! You have no idea of the horrible tricks he played off upon all the lodgers as well as us. Why, just to give you one little proof of his villainy, there was hardly a single wind instrument he did not make use of as a sort of annoyance to the lodgers; from the French horn to the flageolet, he made use of all, and even carried his rascality so far as to play false and to keep blowing the same note for hours together; it was enough to worry one out of one's senses. Well, I suppose there were upwards of twenty different petitions sent to our chief lessee, M. Bras Rouge, to turn the beggar out; and, at last, he was only got rid of by paying him two quarters' rent,—rather droll, is it not, for a landlord to pay his lodger? But,

*Monsieur Pipelet.* by Faustin Betbedder, 1870-71. *Such depictions would have been unthinkable during the Empire.*

bless you, the house was so upset by him that he might have had any price so he would but take himself off; however, he *did* go. And now you suppose we were clear of M. Cabrion? I'll tell you. Next night, about eleven o'clock, I was in bed, when rap, rap, rap, comes to the gate. I pulls up the string,—somebody walks up to my door, 'How do you do, porter?' says a voice; 'will you oblige me with a lock of your hair?' 'Somebody has mistaken the door,' says my wife. So I calls out to the stranger, 'You are wrong, friend, you want next door.' 'I think not,' returns the voice; 'this is No. 17, is it not, and the porter's name is Pipelet? I'm all right; so please to open the door and oblige me with a lock of your beautiful hair.' 'My name is Pipelet, certainly,' answers I. 'Well, then, friend Pipelet, Cabrion has sent me for a piece of your hair; he says he must and he will have it.'"

As Pipelet uttered the last words he gave his head a mournful shake, and, folding his arms, assumed an attitude of martyrlike resolution.

"Do you perceive, sir? He sends to me, his mortal enemy, whom he overwhelmed with insults and continually outraged in every way, to beg a lock of my hair,—a favour which even ladies have been known to refuse to a lover!"

"But, supposing this Cabrion had been as good a lodger as was M. Germain," replied Rodolph, with some difficulty preserving the gravity of countenance, "do you think you might have accorded him the favour?"

"Not to the best lodger that treads shoe-leather would I grant a similar request," replied the man in the flapped hat, waving it majestically over his brows as he spoke; "it is contrary to my principles and habits to give my hair to any one, —only I should have refused with the most scrupulous regard to politeness."

"That is not all," chimed in the porteress. "Only conceive, sir, the abominable conduct of that Cabrion, who, from morning to night, at all hours and at all times, sends a swarm of vagabonds like himself to ask Alfred for a lock of his hair, —always for Cabrion!"

"Ah, monsieur," sighed out poor Pipelet, "had I committed the most atrocious crimes, my sleep could not have been rendered more broken and unrefreshing; scarcely do I fall into a doze than I wake starting with the idea of being called by that cursed Cabrion! I suspect everybody, —in each person who approaches me I see an emissary from my persecutor come to request a lock of my hair. I am losing my good spirits, my temper, and becoming gloomy, suspicious, peevish, and ill-natured. This infernal Cabrion has murdered my whole life!"

And Pipelet heaved so profound a sigh that his hat, vibrating for some time from the consequences of the convulsive shake of the head occasioned thereby, fell forward and completely veiled his care-stricken features.

"I can well understand, now," said Rodolph, "that you are not particularly partial to painters; but I suppose the M. Germain you were praising so highly made up for the bad treatment you received from M. Cabrion?"

"Yes, yes, sir; as I told you, M. Germain was a delightful young man, so honourable and kind-hearted, open as the day, and ever ready to serve and oblige; he was cheerful and merry as need be, but then he always kept his high spirits within proper bounds instead of worrying people to death by his unmeaning hoaxes, like that Cabrion, who I wish was at the devil!"

"Come, come, my good M. Pipelet, I must not let you thus excite yourself; and who, now, is the person fortunate enough to possess such a pattern of a lodger as this M. Germain seems to have been?"

"That is more than I can tell you; no one knows whither he has gone, nor are they likely, except, indeed, through Mlle. Rigolette."

"And who is Mlle. Rigolette?" demanded Rodolph.

"Why, she is a needlewoman, also living on the fourth floor," cried Madame Pipelet; "another pattern lodger, always pays her rent in advance, and keeps her little chamber so nice and clean; then she is well behaved to every one, so merry and happy, like a bird, though, poor thing! very like a caged bird, obliged to work early and late to earn two francs a day, and often not half that, let her try ever so hard."

"How does it happen that Mlle. Rigolette should be the only person entrusted with the secret of M. Germain's present abode?"

"Why, when he was going away, he came to us and said," returned Madame Pipelet, "'I do not expect any letters; but if, by chance, any should come, please to give them to Mlle. Rigolette.' And she is well worthy of his confidence, if his letters were filled with gold; don't you think so, Alfred?"

"The fact is," said the porter, in a severe tone, "that I know no harm of Mlle. Rigolette, excepting her permitting herself to be wheedled over by that vile scamp, Cabrion."

"But you know, Alfred, that nothing more than a few harmless attentions passed between them," interrupted the porteress; "for, though Mlle. Rigolette is as merry as a kitten, she is as prudent and correct as I am myself. You should see the strong bolts she has inside her door; and if her next-door neighbour will make love to her, that is not her fault; it follows as a matter of course when people are so close to each other. It was just the same with the travelling-clerk we had here before Cabrion, and so it was when M. Germain took the room this abominable painter occupied. So, as I say, there is no blame to Mlle. Rigolette; it arises out of the two rooms joining one another so closely,—naturally that brings about a little flirtation, but nothing more."

"So, then, it becomes a matter of course, does it," said Rodolph, "that every one who occupies the apartment I am to have should make love to Mlle. Rigolette?"

"Why, of course, monsieur; how can you be good neighbours without it,—don't you see? Now, imagine yourself lodging in the very next room to a nice, pretty, obliging young person, like Mlle. Rigolette; well, then, young people will be young people, — sometimes you want a light, sometimes a few live coals to kindle up your fire, maybe a little water, — for one is sure always to find plenty of fresh spring water at Mlle. Rigolette's, she is never without it; it is her only luxury, —she is like a little duck, always dabbling in it; and if she does happen to have a little leisure, such a washing down of floors and cleaning of windows! Never the least soil or neglect about either herself or her apartment, and so you will find."

"And so M. Germain, by reason of his close proximity to Mlle. Rigolette, became what you style upon perfectly neighbourly terms with her?"

"Oh, bless you, yes! Why, the two seemed cut out for each other, so young and so good-looking! It was quite a pleasure to look at them as they came down-stairs of a Sunday to take the only walk, poor things! they could afford themselves throughout the week; she dressed in a smart little cap and a gown that cost, probably, not more than twenty-five sous the ell, but made by herself, and that so tastily that it became her as much as though it had been of satin; he, mind ye, dressed and looking like a regular gentleman."

*The cartoonist Sapeck (Eugène Bataille) and the radical activist and songwriter Jules Jouy were both leaders of the vibrant Bohemian Satire community in the 1880s, collaborators of Alphonse Allais and members of the* **Fumistes, Hydropaths, Incoherents, Chat Noir,** *and other groups (see* **Rêvenance** *No. 1–3). Their short-lived, off-the-cuff, joke journal was destined to become entangled in labour arguments for the next thirty years.*

## (Birth of the *Anti-Concierge*)

Hooray! Hooray!

A new paper is born, which responds to a true social need.

A group of disgruntled tenants are going to start up the *Anti-Concierge,* an organ destined to shed light upon the encroachment of citizens in charge of keeping up our houses.

See the "First-Paris" of the new paper:

"The *Anti-Concierge* shall set itself to the work of assembling all the grievances against the so vicious species of Knights of the Cordon.

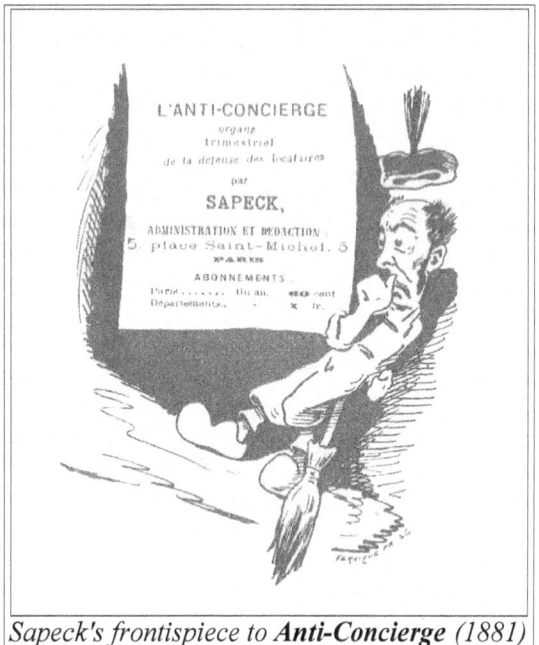

"Harsh, yet just, the *Anti-Concierge* shall have no difficulty recognising that, in the unpleasant corporation which it gives itself the mission of combatting, there exist a few polite and helpful Pipelets, noble exceptions. As for these, the only ones worthy *of panegyrics* (sorry!), we respect them and admire them without reserve. As for the remaining, sad majority, from this moment forward we declare a pitiless war on them, in the name of victimised tenants."

*Sapeck's frontispiece to **Anti-Concierge** (1881)*

You see here the unfortunate pipelet forced to show to his tenants the journal which relates all the long retaliations that he exercises for eleven months out of the year, for the month of December is usually blessed to make everyone forget for the moment blessed with gifts.[18]

Pity our concierges and . . . Let's all subscribe en masse.

by Arthur Verneuil, from *L'Orchestre: Revue quotidienne*, Dec. 10, 1881.

~^~^~^~^~^~^~^~^~^~^~^~^~

## (The Rumours of *Anti-Concierge*'s Death Are Greatly Exaggerated...)

*Note that these short notices were published by the same journal that had printed the satire on the Saint-Simonians translated elsewhere in this issue, albeit after many changes in ownership and management; 27 years later, the **Figaro** would publish Marinetti's **Futurist Manifesto**. Charles Monselet, who made the mistake, was one of the most active historians of the Romanticist avant-garde.*

---

18 étrennes. Christmas gifts, but also tips (in this case, presumably large Christmastime "bonuses").

The journal the *Anti-Concierge* has ceased to appear. You may well have ignored its existence: it was revealed, in fact, by Mr. Charles Monselet. The *Anti-Concierge* had for its founder Mr. Ponchon, one of the last originals.

We owe to him, says Mr. Monselet, several undying tunes, were it only for the very abridged parody of *Adventurers of the Sea*:

> When departing Melun
> We were but one;
> But when we arrived at Carcassonne,
> There wasn't anyone.

~~~~~~~~~~~~~~

[*Correction from three issues later:*]

Mr. Ponchon, the poet, author of the parody of *Adventurers of the Sea* was not at all, it appears, the founder of the journal the *Anti-Concierge*. I was misled by an error of Mr. Monselet.

This vengeful journal had as founders Mr. Jules Jouy and the cartoonist Sapeck, and a letter from M. Jouy, informs me that the *Anti-Concierge* will reappear incessantly.

from *Le Figaro*. Year 28, Series 3, No. 73, Tues. March 14, 1882. & No. 76, Fri. March 17, 1882.

~^~^~^~^~^~^~^~^~^~^~^~

*I am unaware of any surviving copies of Anti-Concierge; here is a description of its contents from an 1888 bibliography of caricature:*

**Anti-Concierge**. Official organ of the defense of tenants. Text by Jules Jouy, drawings by Sapeck. December 1861. 7 issues in-4. On the oversleeves we read: "*The Anti-Concierge* appears on the 1$^{st}$ and the 16$^{th}$ of every month. It intends to draw to public condemnation the overly aggressive pipelets and plead the attenuating circumstances for the reasonable, noble, but rare exceptions in the odious brotherhood of the cordon." Another notice bore: "Non-muzzled concierges are not allowed in the office."

On the fourth page are scattered fantasist announcements of the following kinds: The conciergicide Cabrion, – the heat-conveying Pipeletophobes, – the false pieces to christen and other pleasantries of like calibre.

from J. Grand-Cartaret, *Les Moeurs et la caricature en France.* 1888. La Librairie Illustrée: Paris. p. 559

~^~^~^~^~^~^~^~^~^~^~^~^~^~

## (The Pipelets Unionise!)

*When the Concierges of Paris unionized (in part for reasons that will become clear as this feature continues), Sue's image of Pipelet, coupled with Sapeck's and Jouy's updated versions, became entangled in the debates. The next three articles are from the leftist journal* **The XIX<sup>th</sup> Century,** *published over an eight-year span.*

It seems that Paris is going to possess a new mutual aid society: that of the concierges of the Department of the Seine. Its creation was decided upon in principle at a meeting which took place at the town hall on the rue Drouot. The statutes will be discussed in a later session.

The knights and the knights of the cordon, – who number no less than 16,300 in the Department of the Seine,– already attempted, a dozen years ago, to constitute an analogous society: but they failed. They seem called, this time, for better luck.

Let's hope that they are not too often called to these mandatory assemblies, for the tenants could have to suffer from their too-frequent absences.

On this condition, we consider dignified the tentative encouragements of our bold Pipelets. Only the joyous Sapeck could find it in him to correct it, he who, upon a day of high spirits, launched this journal of vindictive title: the *Anti-Concierge.* But everyone knows that Sapeck, in his administration, became a grave man, said farewell to the fumisteries of yore and long ago renounced his persecution of the gentle porter.[19]

from *Le XIXe Siècle: Journal Républicain*, No. 5478, Dec. 10, 1887. p. 2.

---

19 A tongue-in-cheek reference to Sapeck's short-lived stint as a public servant. Sapeck was a member of the avant-garde satirical group The Fumistes (The Smokers), hence their hijinks as "fumisteries".

~^~^~^~^~^~^~^~^~^~^~^~

## Cost of the Novel in the Porter[20]

Dedicated to the late Sapeck, founder of the *Anti-Concierge.*

The 8[th] Chamber of correctional police, presided over by Mr. Cou[r]urier[21], appeared, yesterday, ferocious toward a concierge who did not think to innovate in slandering two of his tenants.

These two, the husband and the wife, had, in recent years, the misfortune to lose their baby suddenly.

In the presence of the body which had stupified them, the concierge could not stop himself from repeating to every person penetrating the lodge:

— It's not for me to say, but this death isn't natural. For sure, the child must have been poisoned by its parents.

The quarter's police commissioner caught wind of these remarks. An inquest was opened and the child's cadaver transported to the morgue. The autopsy demonstrated that the baby's death was quite natural.

The father and mother sued, yesterday, before the 8th Correction Chamber, the concierge under indictment for defamation. After Mr. Merard's plea for the plaintiffs, the tribunal sentenced the defendant to imprisonment, 100 fr. fine and 500 fr. in damages.

Are you resting easy, Sapeck?

from *Le XIXe Siècle*, No. 9409, Sat. Dec. 14, 1893.

~^~^~^~^~^~^~^~^~^~^~^~

20 The article's title (*Cout du roman chez la portière*) remains obscure.
21 Letter missing in source

# "Anti-Concierge" Jurisprudence

Ah! if the *Anti-Concierge*, whose founder – just punishment or just recompense, as you will, for its polemics – which died to counsel the prefecture[22], was still coming out! What a place of honour it would accord, in its "Our Columns", to the judgement that has been rendered by the Sixth Chamber of the Civil Tribunal of the Seine!

The Sixth Chamber, in fact, has shaken off the yoke of the narrow-minded jurisprudence which has confined itself to declaring that the proprietor is civically responsible for the doings and gestures of his concierge, in the course of fulfilling his functions. In accordance with a famous arrest in the heart of Paris which went all out and ruled the owner of a house civilly responsible for the damage resulting from the infraction of Incitement to Debauchery committed by a concierge in regards to a young underage girl residing in the house, the Sixth Chamber rendered verdict, yesterday, on the pleas of Mr. Lacaze and Mr. Arthur Leymarie, that the action of a concierge to bad-mouth the quality of the merchandise sold by a wine merchant, and, in this instance, to repeat to "his" tenants that the wine sold by the retailer is *skanky,*[23] constitutes a quasi-infraction of which the owner, at fault as the responsible party, owes personal reparation.

While jurisprudence marches merrily on in this matter, the tenants will soon be in a position to pay their rent regularly and exactly with nothing but the offensiveness of the language, well and duly established, of their concierges. This bit of *Litigant's*[24] verse, slightly modified, would then be a continuous reparation:

Bad-mouth me: I have four children to feed . . .

from *Le XIXe siècle: journal quotidien politique et littéraire*, 11 March 1895

~^~^~^~^~^~^~^~^~^~^~^~^~

---

22 A reference to Sapeck leaving the journal to join politics and be elected to the Prefecture of l'Oise.
23 *piquette,* of poor vintage.
24 *Plaideurs.* Capitalised and italicised in the original. Perhaps a journal?

*This militant tract from a Workers' syndicalist paper picks out the **Anti-Concierge** as representative of oppressive stereotypes against labour. **The Hired Help [Le Larbin]** was written by and for labour activists and union members employed in the massive domestic service industries.*

# PLATFORM

## For the Defense of Concierges

The hired-help[25] is the natural friend of the pipelet. Both enveloped in unfair prejudice, they mutually measure the secret of their griefs. You can even say that the distaste which is attached to the profession of concierge is an instance of one prejudged without any reason.

Among the concierges, those who poorly understand their labours are a tiny minority; but the prejudice against all is so strong, that tenants, generally, as soon as they enter a house, consider their porter as a direct enemy, before even meeting him. This absurd prejudice has spread particularly among the writers who, in their fantasist verve,[26] are pleased to furnish the concierge with seven capital sins. Novels and journal articles, all partake in this smear campaign; the concierge has been turned into one of the whipping-boy of modern literature. This bias reached such a pitch, that fifteen years ago two journalists, Jules Jouy and Bataille a.k.a. Sapeck, published a journal, the *Anti-Concierge,* in which the poor parisian pipelets were held up to ridicule, insulted, vilified, dragged through the mud, from the first to the last line of every issue.

To these stupid attacks, the concierges responded with silence, a silence overflowing with dignity. They disdained the calumnies hurled at them by numbskulls, whose real goal was to rake in stacks of money by amusing the gawkers. This attitude, which testifies to a placid world-view, proves that the concierges are wise men. As for their calumniators, the train of events has proven that they were fools: the two editors of the *Anti-Concierge* died, after a few years' interval, each in an insane asylum. That's history, for you!

25 *Larbin*. Derogatory term for domestic servants. This is the title of the magazine, an ironic claiming of the insulting term.

26 *fantasiste*. In the literary terminology of the day, this word referred to the more outré aspects of Romanticism and its descendants, whether flamboyant occultism or (in this case) absurdist humour.

Our main goal is therefore not, in creating this tribune, to go refute the lies which have been thought up to sow the discredit with which concierges have the right to complain. Rather we place our publication at their disposition in order to let them participate in our general inquiry, all defend themselves in it, when an injustice is committed to their detriment. We know, yes, that their modesty usually conceals a heart of gold, frank and loyal friendship, open to all good feelings.

This parisian concierge, whom so many bourgeois imbeciles look at askance, how many times has he, at the peril of his life, grabbed by the throat the burglers who, getting into the house by some trick, were coming down the stairway when the cry: "Stop thief!" rang out, pushed by the terrified tenants? You cannot cite a single porter, who, during any criminal activity, has turned a deaf ear to the appeal: "Help!" The judicial records are, on the contrary, rife with acts of devotion, and show them to us always going to the aid of victims, struggling against the assassin, behaving, in a word, with true heroism . . . And is it not heroic too, these brave concierges who, in these days of anarchist attempts, when they have found at the foot of a wall the criminal engine,[27] about to do its terrible work of destruction, took it fearlessly into their hands, with such coolness and courage, extinguished the wick, doused the explosive in water, and thus saved from a horrible death the tenants of the property confided to their care? . . .

Why then must people forget so easily all these civil traits, so many, which are the honor of this humble association?

As for us, we take it to heart always to render them justice. Let the concierges know clearly: they can, in any situation, just as much for their general defense as in aiding them in their personal vindications against malice and arbitrariness, they can count on our most devoted and most energetic support.

~~~~~~~~~~~~~~~~~~~~

---

27 i.e., a bomb. A string of anarchist bombings and assassinations took place from the 1880s into the 1920s, the first major outbreak of the form of terrorism which has become familiar to us. It is unclear whether this anecdote refers to a specific event, through it was not uncommon for concierges to be wounded in such blasts.

## Syndicalist Chamber of People of Condition

The domestics, who are partisans of the creation of our Syndicalist Chamber, can give us at present their name and address. To do so, they need only write us putting on the envelope: "Mr. Director of Periodical Postage, 14, rue de Baune, in Paris. *Care of the Philosophical Chef*[28]." As soon as we have around fifty members, we will convoke our comrades for a private meeting to listen to them. The members' names will not be communicated to anyone but the provisional committee, composed exclusively of domestics devoted to our work.

from *Le Larbin: Tribune permanente ouverte aux revendications des domestiques.* No. 1. Undated, c.1900, p. 20–22.

~^~^~^~^~^~^~^~^~^~^~^~^~^~^~^~^~^~^~^~^~^~^~^~^~^~^~^~^~^~

*This final entry can be looked at as an add-on to the previous issue's special feature on French dance-club culture in the 1830s–50s. Karr, who wrote and published the satirical proto-Zine* **Les Gûepes** *[The Wasps], will be familiar to regular readers of* **Rêvenance** *(see Nos. 1–3).*

# Random Stuff (1841)

*by Gustave Karr*

In *The Favourite,* presented at the Paris Opera, – there's still a church, – there's now one in every opera. – which must naturally be diverted into two kinds of people, – first the pious people, who don't like that we allow actors such performances. And those who, not going to mass, neither want to discover it upon the boards, where they come looking for something else.

The former like nothing better than to go to mass, – the latter prefer the Musard Ball.

But, everything's mixed up, everything's confounded in a weird Tohu-bohu.[29] – If the Opera,

28 or the Chef Philosopher (*Pour remettre au Couisinier Philosophe.*)
29 An extremely rare word, that was likely current as Romanticist/Bohemian slang (note its resonance with other key argot in the article such as the *cancan,* etc.). It derives from Jewish theology, and denotes the primordial chaos prior to the Word–an idea relating to the theory of Romanticist frenzy, and likely to appeal to the hermetic, quasi-cabalistic elements of the movement.

on certain days, has the air of a church, – we have the church of Notre-Dame-de-Lorette[30], which has the air of an auditorium or ballroom, and which we justifiably dub a Musard church.

It is, every Sunday, the meeting-place of a slew of dancers[31] and all the kept girls[32] of the neighbourhood. – What's more we encounter there a throng of young guys, less punctilious than in yesteryear to the holy services.

That's probably wherefore this church isn't terribly well-formed – why they position so many uniformed policemen there – probably to prevent indecent dances. – They announce a massive ball at Notre-Dame de Paris.

Regarding these indecent dances and policemen, militiamen[33], etc. – who are charged with cracking down, in the public establishments, – on the popular cauchucas[34] and exaggerated fandangos, – aren't they capable of making some huge mistakes? – Recently, a man arrested by them for a like offense, called upon, before the sixth chamber, some embarrassing theories.

–*We have,* said he,

The gracious cancan, – the saint-simonian, – the half-cancan, – the cancan, – the cancan and a half, – and the cahut; – this last dance is is the only one prohibited. I was dancing the gracious cancan.

Wouldn't it be timely to open, for the good of those gentlemen the police and militiamen, a special school of *bizarre* dances, – where they would learn to perfectly discern the specific char-

---

30 This new church had been built by the ruling Orleans monarchy five years previous, which gives the pun a subtle political jibe.

However, Karr is making a pun with Romanticist argot; several months previously, his friend Nestor Roqueplan (a Romanticist humourist) had coined or popularised the slang term "Lorette" to signify a young, lower-class single woman supported as a mistress by a wealthy man. "Lorettes" would often have met their suitors at dance-halls and balls. The term grew in popularity and remained current throughout the century.

The new church was surrounded by cheaply-built new apartments (note Karr's jab at the quality of construction) which, due to a slow-drying plaster that caused respiratory problems, became inhabited by many poor working women, many of whom were susceptible to the advances of wealthier young men: hence the slang term deriving from the neighbourhood. (see Michael Marrinan, *Romantic Paris: Histories of a Cultural Landscape, 1800–1850,* p. 294. Marrinan traces this as the origin of the term, but not to Roqueplan personally.) Roqueplan's coinage is cited in Rigaut's 1888 *Dictionnaire d'argot moderne* (featured in the previous issue), which was compiled and published by collaborators of Alphonse Allais, in whose work Karr's influence is clear.

31 danseuses, female dancers

32 i.e., "lorettes" according to the newly-coined slang term.

33 gardes municipaux

34 See notes to "Partymar with the Badouillards" in *Rêvenance* No. 3.

acteristics of these dances they've had enough of.

@ @ @

Out in the world, when a man has invited a woman to dance who can't accept due to a previous offer, he goes on to another, and it seems to me to be an insult to both women. To the first, he would say thus: "I asked you by chance, without preference; I don't dance with you; so it goes! I'll dance with someone else." – To the second: "I take you for lack of anyone better; if the one whom I invited first had been free, I'd never consider you; she's prettier than you, more elegant, more spiritual than you."

Some people, in order to avoid this, don't dance when the woman whom they've chosen isn't free; – but it can thus come about that they pass the night without dancing, some wish they would have.

Here's how they do it in some of the towns in the Midi:[35] – each man, when coming in, plucks from a basket an artificial flower, – and, when he's going to invite a woman to dance, – in the place of this seldom-varied formula:

"Would Madame like to do me the honour of dancing with me?" he offers her a flower, which she keeps in her waistband until she's danced the promised contradance; – then, the contra-dance over, she returns the bouquet to him, which he'll offer to another. – In this way, they don't run the risk of inviting a woman already spoken for, – because each woman who doesn't have a flower is free and waiting to dance.

*–trans. Olchar E. Lindsann*

from *Les Gûepes*, Janvier 1841. Self-Published: Paris. p. 66–68. <u>from the Revenant Archive.</u>

~^~^~^~^~^~^~^~^~^~^~^~^~^~^~^~^~^~^~^~^~^~^~^~^~^~^~^~^~^~

## A Reminder to Readers

It's not my *goal* to be responsible for 80-90% of each issue's content; I love contributions, whether in the form of responses to text published here (letters, poems, drawings, etc.), edited selections and/or translations of texts, essays on underground history and/or historiography, book reviews, reading lists, etc. etc. etc.! *monoclelash@gmail.com*

---

35 The southern coastal regions of France.

Cham, **Eugène Sue's Romantico-political Candidacy** (1848). By the 1848 Revolution, even mainstream Romanticism was associated with socialism, and like Victor Hugo, the creator of Pipelet, Eugène Sue (see **Mysteries of Paris** in this issue) made the transition into politics, elected to the Chamber of Deputies of the short-lived Second Republic; he was exiled for protesting Napoleon III's coup d'état, dying in Italy. The American Socialist leader and labour organiser Eugene Victor Debs was named after Hugo and Sue. Here he is pictured surrounded by his best-known characters, most drawn from the working or criminal classes. <u>Lithograph from the Revenant Archive.</u>

# Now Available from the mOnocle-Lash Revenants Series

*The Revenant Series imprint publishes translations, histories, and new editions of works related to the 19th Century avant-garde, including the Romanticist, Frenetic, Occultist, Utopian Socialist, Bohemian, Parnassian, Anarchist, Decadent, and Symbolist communities.*

**Baptism : Marriage**, *by The Mapah, Simon Ganneau*, trans. Olchar E. Lindsann. After Romanticist sculptor and phrenologist Simon Ganneau was visited by the spirit of his recently deceased wife, he founded the Evadamiste movement, a hybrid of occultism, gnosticism, feminism, and utopian socialism. Though small, the movement lasted for twenty years and at one time counted many influential activists and occultists among its adherents, including Eliphas Levi, Flora Tristan, Alphonse Esquiros, and Alexandre Dumas. No text of the movement has ever been translated before. This eight-page pamphlet, first published in 1838, proclaims the coming new age, heralded by the androgenous male-female deity Evadam. Supplemented with a contemporary description of the Mapah by the avant-garde satirist Gustave Karr and a portrait by the Evadamist artist Traviès.

**Lycanthropy: Some Shreds Torn from Rhapsodies**, *by Petrus Borel*, trans. O. Lindsann, Joseph Carter, & Raymond E. André III. Petrus Borel played a seminal role in the founding of the avant-garde as a writer, theorist, organiser and public provocateur. Though acknowledged as a major influence by Baudelaire, Lautréamont, Tzara, and Breton, his work is scarcely known even French, and only a scattering of poems have ever been translated into English. This anthology includes five poems from Borel's 1832 collection Rapsodies, with parallel French texts, translators notes, and footnotes unfolding Borel's many references to the Romanticist avant-garde community and its ideological and historical contexts; Borel's Preface to the book, arguably the most influential manifesto of avant-garde Romanticism, heavily annotated; a short critical biography; and a selected bibliography of works in English.

## In Preparation

Coming Jan. 2019: **Cinders from 'Fire and Flame'**, *by Philothée O'Neddy*. New translations from the signature 1833 collection of the Bouzingo co-founder, one of the most influential, yet forgotten, writers of the Romanticist avant-garde. An appetizer for a forthcoming full-length anthology.

**Long-Term Anthologies in Preparation:** Estimated 2020 Release: *The Frenetic Feminine* (Anthology of Female founders of the avant-garde, c.1820–40), *Incoherent Footprints of the Rabid Black Cat* (Anthology of the Hydropathes, Incoherents, and Chat Noir groups c.1880–1900) & an anthology focusing on the role of dancing in the Romanticist Avant-Garde, c.1830–50. Estimated 2021 Release: *Tales of the Bouzingo* (Anthology of the first self-declared Avant-Garde collective, 1829–34).

Oct., A.Da. 102  /  A.H. 188  /  2018 C.E.

**mOnocle-Lash Anti-Press**
# REVENANT SERIES
monoclelash.wordpress.com
monoclelash@gmail.com

# INDEX

*Italicized numerals designate works created, about, or translated by the person, drawn from the source, or focusing on the topic.*

*Topics likely to be of interest to regular readers have been indexed; contact me to suggest index-threads for incorporation in future volumes. Book titles are not included, but the authors of books mentioned are (even if the name does not appear in the text). Authors listed on back cover notices are indexed, but only at first appearance. The pseudo/aristocratic "de" has not been included in alphabetization. Translations by Lindsann are not listed, as default for the publication in these issues.*

180

# Now Available from the mOnocle-Lash
# Revenant Editions Series

*The Revenant Series imprint publishes translations, histories, and new editions of works related to the 19th Century avant-garde, including the Romanticist, Frenetic, Occultist, Utopian Socialist, Bohemian, Parnassian, Anarchist, Decadent, and Symbolist communities.*

*Death To Art,* by Vasilisk Gnedov, translated by Volodymyr Bilyk: The Poet Vasilisk Gnedov was a unique and seminal figure in the Russian Futurist movement, but remains virtually unknown in English. This double translation of Gnedov's minimal 1913 masterpiece by the Ukranian avant-garde poet Volodymyr Bilyk, in which two translations using distinct approaches face off against each other and meet in the book's centerfold, reveal both Gnedov's linguistic playfulness and his previously-unnoticed interventions of the Ukrainian language into his primarily Russian texts. In these poems, language is compressed past the point which syntax or even words can support, and new crystalline units of language glisten up at us from the page. With a tipped-in biographical introduction by the translator.

18 pgs. on folded 8.5" x 11".  1813 / Oct., 2019          $2.75 + 1.00 s/h

*Baptism : Marriage, by The Mapah, Simon Ganneau,* trans. Olchar E. Lindsann. The Evadamistes formulated a wildly eccentric hybrid of occultism, gnosticism, feminism, and utopian socialism. Though small, the movement lasted for twenty years and at one time counted many influential activists and occultists among its adherents, including Eliphas Levi, Flora Tristan, Alphonse Esquiros, and Alexandre Dumas. No text of the movement has ever been translated before. This eight-page pamphlet, first published in 1838, proclaims the coming new age, heralded by the androgenous male-female deity Evadam. Supplemented with a contemporary description of the Mapah by the avant-garde satirist Gustave Karr and a portrait by the Evadamist artist Traviès.

8 pgs. on folded 8.5" x 11".  1832-91 / Sept., 2016          $1.00 + 1.00 s/h

***Lycanthropy: Some Shreds Torn from Rhapsodies***, *by Petrus Borel*, trans. O. Lindsann, Joseph Carter, & Raymond E. André III. Petrus Borel played a seminal role in the founding of the avant-garde as a writer, theorist, organiser and public provocateur. Though acknowledged as a major influence by Baudelaire, Lautréamont, Tzara, and Breton, his work is scarcely known even French, and only a scattering of poems have ever been translated into English. This anthology includes five poems from Borel's 1832 collection Rapsodies, with parallel French texts, translators notes, and footnotes unfolding Borel's many references to the Romanticist avant-garde community and its ideological and historical contexts; Borel's Preface to the book, arguably the most influential manifesto of avant-garde Romanticism, heavily annotated; a short critical biography; and a selected bibliography of works in English.

*36 pgs. on folded 8.5"x11". Jan., 1832 / Aug., 2014*      *$2.50 + 1.00 s/h or trade.*

***Pif Paf Patapan! A Sampler of Phonetic Poetry From the 19th Century***, *by ThéophileGautier, Charles Nodier, Paul Verlaine, & Francis Vielé-Griffin.* A pocket pre-history of sound poetry: five phonetic poems published between 1830 & 1891. The poets who were read by the Futurists, Dadas, & Zoumists, and whose experiments they consolidated into a new form.

8 pgs on folded 8.5" x 11". 1832-91 / Sept., 2016      $1.00 + 1.00 s/h

***The Garrick Remedy***, *by Joseph Bouchardy, Translated by Talia Felix.* Though virtually forgotten today, Joseph Bouchardy (1810-1870) was a co-founder of the Jeunes-France / Bouzingo group. This drole tale, written in 1835 on the cusp of Bouchardy's switch from engraving to drama, is his first work ever translated into English. In it, Lady Anna has fallen in love at a performance of Romeo and Juliet—but does she love the famous Romantic actor Garrick, or the character of Romeo, or the play itself? In any case, her father has offered £20,000 to anyone who can cure her infatuation. Bouchardy swings the reader deviously back and forth between wistful sentiment and disillusioned irony. He also sheds some light on Romanticist attitudes toward theatre, history, truth, fiction, and the blending of life and art.

36 pgs. on folded 8.5"x11". 1835-36 / Sept. 2015      $2.50 + 1.00 s/h

**Bouzingo Anti-Translations**, *from the Kohoutenberg Institute for Research and Application*

Homophonic, google-skewed, and alinear anti-translations from our colleagues in Kohoutenberg. Retorico Unentesi, Feito Zahlt, Augen Konne, and Poss Facrienci show us what the Bouzingo might be writing if they'd come to age in the early 21st rather than early 19th Century avant-garde.

*8 p. on double-folded 8.5 x 11.    4 for $1.00*

**Revenant Anti-Bios (Largely-Truish Histories of the Avant-Garde)**, *by Olchar Lindsann.*

The Anti-Bio Series (or Largely-Trueish-Histories) offer short, humorous, usually stupid, sometimes fantastically embellished biographies of little-known, largely forgotten avant-gardists from the past two centuries (with a few well-known people thrown in too). Each is 8 pages long, hastily made in less than three hours from conception to printing, and costs only 50 cents. They are appetizers, and readers are encouraged to fact-check, explore, and do a bit more research themselves. Collect them all!

#1: Tristan Tzara: King of the Aardvarks
#2: Gérard de Nerval: A Tragedy
#3: Raymond Roussel: Taxi-Driver of the Stars
#4: Célestin Nanteuil: Time-Traveler of the Avant-Garde
#5: Joseph Bouchardy: Playwright of Murder and Confusion!
#6: Laurent Tailhade: Decadent, Anarchist, Avant-Victim
#7: George Sand: Gender-Bender of the 19th Century
#8: The Chevalier de Saint-Georges: Composer, Swordsman, Revolutionary Soldier, Ex-Slave, &
             the Most famous black Frenchman of the 18th Century!
#9: The Chevalier d'Eon: Intersexed Spy of the 18th Century

*Two for $1.00 + 0.50 s/h OR #1-8  for $4.00 + $1.25 s/h*

Forthcoming from

# Revenant Editions

### Translations, Republications, & Commentaries
### on the 19<sup>th</sup> Century Avant-Garde & Radical Culture

*Père Ubu's Almanac, by Alfred Jarry, translated by Amy Oliver.* (Dis-]orient yourself toward the coming 'pataphysico-symbolico-hermetico-bohemian year with a new, comedically on-point translation of Jarry's 1899 annual by the British Post-NeoAbsurdist Amy Oliver. The book's original formatting and layout, a thorough parody and détourne of the positivist Almanacs that permeated the 19<sup>th</sup> Century, will be reproduced as closely as possible.

*Selected Dada Texts (Title Undetermined), by Georges Ribemont-Dessaignes, translated by Olchar E. Lindsann.* One of the most ferociously outspoken and aggressively nonsensical of the Paris Dadas, Ribemont-Dessaignes' work has appeared only piecemeal in English. This chapbook will include poems, essays, manifestos, and "dramatic" scenes from his Dada period.

*Selected Bouzingo Texts (Title Undetermined).* A sampler of poems, manifestos, stories, etchings, drawings, and lithographs by members of the Jeunes-France, aka Petit-Cénacle, aka Bouzingo group – the first self-described avant-garde cultural collective and a major model for the Dada and Surrealist movements. A hefty chapbook preview of a full-length anthology farther down the line. Includes work by Petrus Borel, Théophile O'Neddy, Théophile Gautier, Gérard de Nerval, Joseph Bouchardy, Augustus MacKeat, Célestin Nanteuil, Achille Devéria, Louis Boulanger, Eugène Devéria, Jehan Duseigneur, Alphonse Brot, Napoleon Thom, Léon Clopet – most of the texts translated for the first time, many images reproduced in book form for the first time in a century.

## Long-Term Anthologies in Preparation:

**Estimated 2022 Release:** *The Frenetic Feminine [Working Title].* Texts and images by over a dozen female co-founders of the avant-garde, 1820–1840, many appearing in English for the first time. Including Sand, de Staël, Mercoeur, Debordes-Valmore, Argoult, Tastu, Waldor, Gay, Girardin, de Salm, and others.

& an anthology focusing on the role of dancing in the Romanticist Avant-Garde, c.1830–50. **Estimated 2023 Release:** *Tales of the Bouzingo* (Full-lengthnthology of the first self-declared Avant-Garde collective, 1829–34).

**Available as they appear along with** other disorienting works by fascinating dead people:
*Order at  www.monoclelash.wordpress.com/revenant-editions/*

www.ingramcontent.com/pod-product-compliance
Lightning Source LLC
Chambersburg PA
CBHW080729020726
47503CB00010B/2850